Corporate Acquisitions and Mergers in Canada

Corporate Acquisitions and Mergers in Canada

Fifth Edition

Danny Wakeling
Ahad Ahmed

Dentons Canada LLP

This book was originally published as a chapter in Corporate Acquisitions and Mergers.

General Editor: Peter Begg

Wolters Kluwer

Published by:
Kluwer Law International B.V.
PO Box 316
2400 AH Alphen aan den Rijn
The Netherlands
E-mail: lrs-sales@wolterskluwer.com
Website: www.wolterskluwer.com/en/solutions/kluwerlawinternational

Sold and distributed by:
Wolters Kluwer Legal & Regulatory U.S.
920 Links Avenue
Landisville, PA 17538
United States of America
E-mail: customer.service@wolterskluwer.com

ISBN 978-94-035-1209-9

e-Book: ISBN 978-94-035-1219-8
web-PDF: ISBN 978-94-035-1229-7

Contents

Dentons Canada LLP

Dentons is the world's largest law firm, delivering quality and value to clients around the globe. Dentons is a leader on the Acritas Global Elite Brand Index, a BTI Client Service 30 Award winner and recognized by prominent business and legal publications for its innovations in client service, including founding Nextlaw Labs and the Nextlaw Global Referral Network. Dentons' polycentric approach and world-class talent challenge the status quo to advance client interests in the communities in which we live and work. www.dentons.com

Authors

Ahad Ahmed is a senior associate in the Toronto Office of Dentons. His practice focuses on mergers and acquisitions (M&A), private equity, corporate finance and commercial matters. Ahad has significant experience in domestic and cross-border M&A, reorganization, restructuring and financing transactions.

Danny Wakeling is a partner in Dentons' Corporate group and co-leader of our national Mergers and Acquisitions group in Canada. His practice consists of broad-based transactional work with an emphasis on mergers and acquisitions, capital markets and corporate finance. Danny represents a range of public and private companies in various share and asset transactions, strategic investments, capital raising, and general corporate and governance matters.

The authors wish to recognize the contributions of current and former colleagues, including, Alberto Slinger, Camila Maldi, Adam Goodman, Daniel Safi, Emily Kroboth, Heidi Clark, Ife Adebola, Jamie Cardy, Jonathan Mor, Kurtis Parcells, Larry Nevsky, Larysa Workewych, Luca Lucarini, Mariam Momodu, Matthew Fleming, Noah Walters, Paige Donnelly, Rocky Swanson, Sara-Ann Wilson, Sarah Lam, Sean Stephenson, Simon Kupi, and Tamara Galstyan in reviewing and providing content for this chapter. In addition, the authors would like to recognize the work of the previous authors of the Canadian chapter, Kelli Patel and Vivian Poon, whose previous contributions provided an invaluable guide to the current version of this publication.

Currency & Notice

Mergers & Acquisitions in Canada reflects Canadian laws as of 31 July 2024, without regard to amendments not yet in force. Although the authors cover numerous legal issues that may arise in the course of mergers and acquisitions, this publication provides general information only, is not a complete statement of applicable law and considerations in embarking on Canadian mergers and acquisitions, and is not intended and does not provide legal advice to the readers. Readers should consult with lawyers qualified in Canadian law with respect to particular issues and specific transactions and should not rely upon this publication. Subject to appropriately conducted conflict checks and formal retainer agreements, Dentons would be pleased to provide assistance to readers with respect to mergers and acquisition transactions or any issues discussed in this publication.

A Note on Conventions

For ease of exposition, the author has adopted certain conventions:

- Unless otherwise noted, the discussion is focused on the *Canada Business Corporations Act* (CBCA), which is the federal business incorporation statute and representative of the main form of business corporation statute in Canada.
- The discussion of securities laws and regulations governing offering corporations is focused on the Province of Ontario. Most offering corporations in Canada will be registered with the Ontario Securities Commission and subject to the *Securities Act* (Ontario).
- Unless otherwise noted, references to 'provinces' include the three territories of Canada.

Monetary figures are provided in Canadian currency.

Canadian Offices

CALGARY

15th Floor, Bankers Court

850 – 2nd Street SW

Calgary, Alberta T2P 0R8

Tel.: 403 268 7000

Fax: 403 268 3100

EDMONTON

2500 Stantec Tower

10220 – 103 Avenue NW

Edmonton, Alberta T5J 0K4

Tel.: 780 423 7100

Fax: 780 423 7276

MONTRÉAL

39th Floor, 1 Place Ville-Marie

Montréal, QC H3B 4M7

Tel.: 514 878 8800

Fax: 514 866 2241

OTTAWA

99 Bank Street

Suite 1420
Ottawa, ON K1P 1H4
Tel.: 613 783 9600
Fax: 613 783 9690

TORONTO

77 King Street West, Suite 400
Toronto-Dominion Centre
Toronto, ON, M5K 0A1
Tel.: 416 863 4511
Fax: 416 863 4592

VANCOUVER

20th Floor, 250 Howe Street
Vancouver, BC V6C 3R8
Tel.: 604 687 4460
Fax: 604 683 5214

1 LOCAL, ECONOMIC AND CULTURAL ASPECTS

[01] This section describes the structure of the Canadian legal environment in which mergers and acquisitions take place.

1.1 Profile

[02] Canada is located in the northern part of the continent of North America. It is the second-largest country by land mass and is rich in natural resources. Canada is bounded by three oceans: the Arctic Ocean in the north, the Pacific Ocean in the west and the Atlantic Ocean in the east. Canada's southern border is shared with the United States (US) and follows the 49th parallel for much of the west and mid-west. Canada's border with the US constitutes the longest land border between two countries. Canada's largest trading partners are the US, China, the United Kingdom (UK) and the European Union (EU).

[03] Canada's total population is approximately 41 m. In recent years, Canada's population growth has been the highest among the G-7 countries. The increase in Canada's population is driven by immigration. Nevertheless, in stark contrast to its geographical size, Canada remains the least populous country in the G-7 and has historically been only one-tenth of the total population of the US. According to the latest figures released by the Government of Canada in July 2024, Canada's labour force currently has 21 883 000 participants.

[04] Canada's two official languages are French and English. The official currency is the Canadian dollar.

1.2 Government and Political System

[05] Canada is a federal state in which executive and legislative functions are divided between a national or federal Parliament and ten provincial legislatures. In addition, Canada contains three northern territories, which are creatures of federal statute but have delegated legislative authority similar to provinces. In addition, municipal governments exercise delegated legislative authority by provincial statute. In some cases, Canada's aboriginal groups have limited self-governing rights as a result of treaties or other agreements.

[06] The subject-matters over which Canada's federal Parliament and provincial legislatures have authority are generally intended to be mutually exclusive. Parliament has jurisdiction over international trade, foreign investment, banking, interprovincial trade, harbours and aeronautics, interprovincial railways, telecommunications, intellectual property, citizenship and immigration, and criminal law (among other things). Provincial legislatures have jurisdiction over natural resources, land use, property rights, and civil rights (such as contracts, torts and most other types of private law).

[07] Although the powers of Parliament and the legislatures are intended to be mutually exclusive, there is significant overlap because these entities may regulate different aspects of a commercial activity. If there is an operational conflict between federal law and provincial law, federal law will govern to the extent of the conflict.

[08] Canada is a politically stable country that is generally welcoming of foreign investment, although there are certain industries in which foreign ownership may be limited or otherwise regulated. Canada is also a member of the World Trade Organization (WTO) and a party to the United States-Mexico-Canada Agreement (USMCA) as well as other bilateral Foreign Investment Promotion and Protection Agreements (FIPPAs). Canada is also a party to the Trans-Pacific Partnership agreement and has ratified the International Centre for Settlement of Investment Disputes (ICSID) Convention on the Settlement of Investment Disputes. Canada is a member of the G-7 and G-20 nations and is well-integrated into the global financial system.

1.3 Legal System

[09] In all provinces other than Québec, private law (property and civil rights) is based on the English common law tradition. In Québec, private law is based on the French civil law tradition. Public law, in all provinces, is based on the English common law tradition.

[10] Federally, Canada is officially bilingual. French is the sole official language in Québec. New Brunswick and the Territories are officially bilingual. In addition, the Territories officially recognize certain aboriginal languages. In other jurisdictions, English is the predominant language.

[11] Parliament, the provincial legislatures and the territorial legislatures each have the power to incorporate business corporations. Federal corporations have the right to carry on business throughout Canada. Although the provincial power of incorporation is constitutionally limited to corporations having 'provincial objects', this restriction has been narrowly construed. Provincial business corporation statutes permit a corporation to carry on business outside of the province subject to the laws of the other jurisdiction. Typically, a company incorporated in one province must extra-provincially register in the other province in order to carry on business. A similar rule applies to foreign corporations seeking to carry on business in a province.

[12] The internal governance of a corporation is generally a matter that is regulated by the legislation under which the corporation was incorporated. Matters relating to the governance of a provincial or territorial business corporation will be brought before the courts of the province or territory of incorporation. Matters relating to the governance of a federal business corporation may be brought before any provincial or territorial superior court.

[13] Parliament and provincial legislatures have the power to regulate corporations engaged in activities that otherwise fall within the jurisdiction of those legislative bodies. Canada's public capital markets are regulated provincially, with significant cooperation and coordination between provincial regulators. Although there has been ongoing discussion of the creation of a national securities regulator, the Supreme Court of Canada has concluded that the day-to-day regulation of all aspects of contracts for securities would go beyond the power of Canada's federal Parliament, although it would be possible for Parliament to regulate matters of genuine national importance and scope such as managing systemic risk.

[14] The Canadian *Charter of Rights and Freedoms* (the 'Charter') is part of Canada's constitution. The Charter imposes limitations on Parliament and the legislatures and administrative bodies created under the legislative authority of Parliament and the legislatures. The Charter guarantees certain fundamental rights and freedoms for all persons in Canada as well as guaranteeing certain aboriginal rights, which will be discussed in subsequent sections.

[15] Corporations may obtain the protection of the Charter in certain areas. For example, a corporation may assert that a law is unlawful if it would infringe on the rights of a natural person. Importantly, corporations may rely on the Charter in respect of unreasonable searches and seizures by governmental authorities.

[16] The independence of the judiciary in Canada facilitates the effective enforcement of Canadian laws in the courts. Contractual and other obligations are enforced by commencing judicial proceedings in a provincial superior court of competent jurisdiction. Generally, private companies may enforce their contractual agreements against governmental agencies or Ministries of the federal, provincial or territorial governments (i.e., the Crown or Crown agents) through the courts. No permission of the government is required; however, in many cases, advance notice must be given to the government before commencing a proceeding. When contracting with the Crown or Crown agents, organizations should be mindful that statutes of general application may not apply to the Crown or Crown agents without an express indication to that effect in the statute.

[17] Public companies in Canada are subject to continuous disclosure requirements. As a result, material information relating to potential public company targets may be found through public resources. The most significant resource for locating information about a public company is through the System for Electronic Document Analysis and Retrieval (SEDAR+) filing system maintained by the Canadian Securities Administrators (CSA). Documents that are required to be filed with securities regulators in Canada must be posted to SEDAR+. These include comprehensive annual information forms (AIFs), quarterly and annual financial statements and management discussion and analysis, as well as press releases regarding material changes.

[18] Private companies have no obligation to publicly disclose information about their financial and business affairs. It is very uncommon for them to do so. Nevertheless, research and consultancy firms are able to assist clients in identifying and researching potential acquisition targets.

1.4 Current Economic Aspects

[19] Like many other countries around the world, increased levels of inflation and the after-effects of regional conflicts such as the Russia-Ukraine war have had a major impact on the Canadian economy. Abnormally high levels of inflation have brought a level of unpredictability and, when combined with higher interest rates, there has been a noticeable impact on consumer behaviour and confidence. M&A activity has correspondingly slowed since its peak in 2021. There were 2 661 M&A deals in Canada in 2023 with an aggregate value of CAD287 bn, which represents 65% of deal volume and 51% of deal value from 2021's peak. Indicators suggest that Canada's outlook for M&A activity is expected to increase and be commensurate with pre-peak levels.

[20] In addition, Canada has a friendly environment in which to restructure distressed businesses. The federal Companies' Creditors Arrangement Act (CCAA) provides a flexible legislative structure for companies to restructure their arrangements with creditors and sell non-core assets under protection and supervision of the court. The CCAA is available to companies that are insolvent (on a balance sheet test or otherwise unable to pay their creditors as their debts become due) and who have liabilities over CAD5 m. In some cases, companies may liquidate through proceedings conducted under this legislation. Recent examples of the use of this legislation include the restructuring of Pride Group, one of the largest trucking carriers in Canada, and Ted Baker, a conglomerate of companies operating a fashion clothing and accessories retail business. The Office of the Superintendent of Bankruptcy Canada maintains an online list of all companies granted protection under the CCAA. The list is updated within two business days of an order granting protection.

[21] Unemployment rates have fluctuated in recent years but remain within a comparatively stable range. The underlying trends for Canada's labour market include an ageing population, reliance on immigration and temporary foreign workers and skills shortages in certain sectors. Canadian provinces and territories have legislation that regulates the minimum wage. Most provinces have set a minimum wage that exceeds CAD15 per hour.

1.5 Main Industries

[22] Canada has abundant natural resources. Canada has one of the largest oil reserves in the world. The vast majority of these reserves are located in Canada's oil sands in the northern area of the Province of Alberta, and, to a lesser extent, in the adjacent province of Saskatchewan. The oil sands take their name from the fact that the crude oil deposit is suspended in a mixture of sand, clay and water. Most of the reserves consist of bitumen, which is heavy crude oil. The bitumen cannot be shipped by pipeline without being diluted with other hydrocarbons or by 'upgrading' the bitumen into lighter crude. The Trans Mountain Corporation, a Canadian crown corporation, completed construction of the Trans Mountain pipeline extension in May 2024, which substantially expands the capacity to transport oil from Alberta to the Pacific coast. At present, the majority of Canada's oil sands production is exported to the US, frequently by rail.

[23] Canada's oil sands are subject to a number of environmental controls. The majority of oil sands lie too deep to be mined. Instead, these reserves are recovered by drilling wells and then using steam to liquefy the bitumen, which is then pumped to the surface. There are a number of technologies, but these extraction techniques use a significant amount of water. There are environmental limits on the amount of water that may be taken from the local Athabasca River and production water must be transferred to tailings ponds and reused. Companies are also required to reclaim all land after development so that the land is returned to boreal forest. The industry has been working to reduce Canada's greenhouse gas emissions per barrel of oil produced.

[24] Canada also has abundant natural gas resources across the country. Currently, much of the conventional natural gas production is located in the provinces of British Columbia, Alberta and Saskatchewan and offshore in the Maritimes on the east coast of Canada. Canada has become one of the top six largest producers of natural gas in the world. Canada has an extensive natural gas pipeline system, including distribution pipes directly to homes and businesses. Some estimates are that nearly 393 m cubic metres of gas move through Canadian pipelines each day. Because Canada's natural gas frequently contains high levels of hydrogen sulphide (sour gas), Canada has become a leader in the operation of sour gas facilities.

[25] Canada estimates that it has approximately 367 m hectares of wooded land representing approximately 9% of the world's forests and 36% of the world's certified forested area. Canada is among the largest forest products exporters. The forestry industry is concentrated principally in British Columbia, Quebec and Ontario. Most of Canada's forested land is publicly owned Crown land under federal, provincial or territorial jurisdiction and harvested under forest or timber licences.

[26] Canada also has one of the most diverse and productive fisheries in the world. Canada ranks among the top fish and seafood exporters, with the majority of exports destined for the US. Canada's fishery is primarily regulated by the Department of Fisheries and Oceans Canada to ensure the sustainability of the fishery. The Canadian Food Inspection Agency provides export certification.

[27] It should be noted that some of these industries are subject to restrictions on foreign ownership. For more information on such restrictions, please see the section on 'Restricted Sectors'.

[28] Although resource-rich, Canada has made significant private sector and public sector investments in the technology sector, including information technology, biotechnology, agricultural technology and clean technology businesses. Canada continues to have a vibrant technology sector.

[29] Canada has extensive transportation industries in Canada including, rail, aerospace and maritime shipping. Canada has two major transcontinental freight railways owned and operated by the Canadian National Railway and the Canadian Pacific Railway. The Canadian aerospace industry is a significant part of the Canadian economy and includes research and development, manufacturing and export of aircraft, engines and components. Canada has numerous international airports through which Canadian goods and services are shipped and which transport passengers within Canada and to major cities around the world. Canada has several major ports in Canada, including Vancouver (British Columbia), Montréal (Québec) and Halifax (Nova Scotia), with Canadian ports handling more than 345 m tonnes of cargo annually.

1.6 Cultural Aspects

[30] Although Canada has a relatively small population, it is a highly urbanized country. Nearly one in three Canadians live in one of three cities: Toronto (Ontario), Montréal (Québec) and Vancouver (British Columbia). Other populous cities include Calgary (Alberta), Mississauga (Ontario), Surrey (British Columbia), Laval (Québec), Longueuil (Québec), and Burnaby (British Columbia). Canada's central east provinces of Ontario and Québec have historically been the most populous (and remain so) while metropolitan areas in western Canada have grown beyond the national average in recent years.

[31] Federally, Canada has two official languages – English and French. French is the official language of the Province of Québec. New Brunswick is officially bilingual. English is the predominant language outside of Quebec and New Brunswick. However, there are significant francophone communities in Ontario, Alberta and Manitoba. A number of aboriginal languages are official languages in some of Canada's northern territories. Canada's policy of celebrating and supporting multiculturalism has contributed to the use of a number of other language groups in Canada, particularly in metropolitan areas. Among these are Cantonese, Mandarin, Punjabi, Tagalog, Spanish, Italian, German and Arabic.

[32] Canada has participated in the Organisation for Economic Co-operation and Development (OECD) Program for International Student Assessment, which examines the ability of 15-year-olds to extrapolate and apply knowledge in reading, mathematics and science. The 2018 data set placed Canada 6th in reading performance, 7th in science performance and 9th in mathematics performance.

[33] Business etiquette in Canada involves direct communication and respecting everyone's opinion (regardless of rank or status). Business hours are generally between 9:00 am and 5:00 pm, with a preference for morning appointments. In business meetings, a handshake is the appropriate greeting and should be accompanied by eye-contact. It is common to attend business lunches in Canada. These lunches are relatively short with lighter types of food and little to no alcohol. Standard table manners apply in Canada, and care should be taken not to commence eating until everyone has been served. Although the giving and accepting of gifts is not a normal feature of business transactions, gifts may be offered after completing a transaction subject to any policies that the respective parties have in place. In this case, gifts are unwrapped immediately and shown to everyone. There are no local or established business practices that might represent a hurdle to foreigners.

[34] The cost of doing business in Canada has decreased in recent years with the decline of the Canadian dollar. It is also not a risky place for business transactions given the strong protection for foreign investment and commercial transactions through the establishment of various investment protection regimes and judicial enforcement mechanisms.

2 THE REGULATORY FRAMEWORK

2.1 Business Vehicles

[35] The most common form of business organization for companies with significant assets is a business corporation with limited shareholder liability. However, certain Canadian jurisdictions, namely British Columbia, Alberta and Nova Scotia, permit the incorporation of companies with unlimited shareholder liability. In addition, general partnerships (also known as ordinary partnerships) and limited partnerships may be used for regulatory or tax advantages.

[36] Foreign companies looking to carry on a business in Canada can choose to either incorporate a subsidiary under the federal or provincial statutes or they can obtain a licence and open a Canadian branch. A subsidiary will be subject to the corporate laws in the jurisdiction under which it is incorporated. The new entity will have the flexibility and the facility to carry on business throughout Canada, subject to complying with registration and/or licensing requirements of any particular province in which the subsidiary proposes to carry on business.

2.1.1 Corporate Form

[37] The *Canada Business Corporations Act* (CBCA) is the federal statute governing the incorporation of business corporations and is based on the articles of incorporation model found in the US. Provincial statutes of incorporation in all of the provinces other than Nova Scotia are similar to (and in some cases are modelled on) but not identical with the CBCA. Nova Scotia's *Companies Act* is based on the 'articles and memorandum' model and is derived substantially from the U.K. *Companies Act of 1862*.

[38] A corporation in Canada is recognized as a legal person distinct from its shareholders and management and has potentially a perpetual existence. It has rights and obligations that are similar to a natural person. Business corporations may generally carry on any legal business, hold real and intangible property, enter into contracts and incur liability for contractual and non-contractual obligations. Shareholders are the 'owners' of the corporation and at least one class of shareholders must have the right to vote for the appointment of a board of directors. In a limited liability corporation, which is the predominant form, the shareholders' liability is limited to the amount of their capital investment or, in some instances, the supervision of management in a corporation.

2.1.2 Public Versus Private

[39] Public corporations (often called 'offering corporations') are those whose shares are generally more widely held and the shares of such corporations are often listed on a stock exchange. By contrast, private corporations generally have fewer than fifty shareholders and carry restrictions on the right to transfer the shares of the corporation (the most common restriction is obtaining the consent of a majority of the directors or the shareholders to any proposed sale or transfer of share), and expressly prohibit any invitation to the public to subscribe for securities of the corporation. Only public corporations are required to file public financial statements. Most corporations in Canada are private corporations.

2.1.3 Choice of Jurisdiction of Incorporation

[40] Companies incorporated pursuant to the CBCA have the right to carry on business anywhere in Canada. However, they are subject to the laws of general provincial application, including licensing and registration requirements. A federal registration offers name protection since the name of a federal corporation may be used lawfully in any province or territory in Canada and precludes registration of the same name by anyone else. This name protection is, however, limited and does not prohibit the registration of similar names.

[41] The principal factors in choosing a jurisdiction of incorporation are the following:

- *Residency of Directors*. The CBCA provides that 25% of the directors must be resident Canadians unless there are less than four directors, in which case at least one must be a resident Canadian. Similar requirements are also needed in Manitoba, Newfoundland and Saskatchewan. All other jurisdictions do not require any of the directors to be Canadian residents.
- *Squeeze-Out Transactions*. The CBCA permits the squeeze-out of shareholders of private corporations. Some provincial corporations' statutes, such as in Ontario, do not. This makes the ability to squeeze out minority shareholders more complex and expensive.
- *Proxy Solicitation*. The CBCA requires a company to solicit proxies if it has more than fifty shareholders (two or more joint holders being counted as one shareholder) even if it is not a public corporation. The same rule does not apply in Ontario for private, non-offering corporations.
- *Business Presence*. As a practical matter, unless incorporated federally, a corporation may wish to incorporate in the province or territory in which it will principally conduct its business for administrative convenience or as a result of licensing requirements.

2.1.4 Capitalization

[42] Corporations may be capitalized by equity, debt and, upon operation, retained earnings. Equity or share capital is the amount invested by the shareholders. Debt is the amount that the corporation has borrowed from its creditors. The distinction between debt and equity may be blurred. Some instruments, such as preference shares may have features of debt and equity. Whether an instrument is a debt or equity will be important in the event of insolvency (since debt must be repaid in priority to equity) and will turn on an examination of the features of the instrument rather than the label applied to the instrument.

There are no minimum capitalization requirements. However, there are thin capitalization rules for the computation of income for income tax purposes.

Annual Filing and Reporting Requirements under Corporate Law

[43] The CBCA requires an annual meeting of shareholders (or written resolution of all of the shareholders in lieu of a meeting) at which the shareholders will, among other things, approve the annual financial statements, elect directors, and appoint auditors for the following year. Typically, tightly controlled foreign subsidiaries will use a written resolution in lieu of a meeting in order to conduct this annual business.

[44] Corporations have a number of annual filing obligations in addition to filing returns relating to income tax and commodity taxes and continuous disclosure obligations under securities legislation.

[45] A corporation must file an annual return relating to information about the structure and governance of the corporation. This information is then made available to the public through government registries. Under the CBCA, the annual return must be filed within sixty days of the corporation's anniversary of incorporation. The annual return must provide the date of the last annual meeting of shareholders.

[46] Corporations must also update any changes to their registered office within fifteen days of making a change. The registered office address cannot be a post office box and must be within the province or territory set out in the articles of the corporation. Provincial corporations' legislation have more restrictive rules.

[47] Corporations must also report who the directors are of the corporation. Any changes to the directors and their addresses must be reported to the registrar.

[48] In addition, any changes to a corporation's articles must be filed with the registrar. Changes could include changes to the corporate name, the province or territory in which the registered office is located, the minimum or maximum number of directors, restrictions on the transfer of shares, maximum number and classes of shares, and other fundamental changes to the structure of the corporation as set out in the articles.

[49] Failure to keep a corporation's filings current may result in the corporation being dissolved and all property escheating to the Crown. If a corporation is administratively dissolved, there are procedures for reviving the corporation and restoring all of its rights, property and liabilities. To qualify for revival, the persons seeking revival of the corporation must bring the corporation back into compliance with its obligations regarding information returns and tax filings.

[50] In addition to corporate filings, there are numerous statutes that may require a corporation or other entity to file reports with the government. These may include reports on how the organization is meeting accessibility standards in Ontario for customer service, transportation, information and communications, built environments and employment, as well as employee health and safety.

2.1.5 Ongoing Securities Law Requirements for Public Companies

Registration

[51] Canadian securities law requires that any person engaging in (or holding oneself out as engaging in) trading activity as a business must comply with dealer registration requirements. Any person engaging in trading activity as a business must be registered with the securities regulator in each province or territory where they do business unless an exemption applies. These regulations exist to protect investors by ensuring that dealers have the necessary proficiency, insurance requirements, internal controls and meet the continuing compliance requirements for registrants.

[52] There are a limited number of exemptions from the registration requirements available to certain types of market participants. The most common exemption is for participants making trades solely through a registered dealer.

Prospectus Requirements

[53] Prior to soliciting expressions of interest for the purchase of a distribution of securities, an issuer must, subject to certain exemptions, prepare and file a preliminary prospectus with the relevant securities commissions. Prior to the distribution of securities (in the absence of an exemption), the issuer must file and have approved a final prospectus. A distribution includes an original issue of securities by an issuer as well as a trade in previously issued securities from a 'control block', and certain trades in previously issued securities that were originally issued in reliance upon an exemption from the prospectus requirements.

[54] A prospectus describes the security being issued and the business and affairs of the issuer. It is a comprehensive disclosure document and must contain prescribed information. For distributions made in Québec, the prospectus must be prepared in French, or in French and English.

[55] A misrepresentation in a prospectus for an offering may result in the security holder purchasing in that offering having a right to rescission or a right to damages without proving reliance on the misrepresentation. Security holders who purchased the securities directly from the issuer, upon the securities being issued, are entitled to choose between rescission and an award of damages as a remedy for the misrepresentation. This is known as 'primary market liability'. Security holders who traded on the market in the securities during the period of the misrepresentation may have a right to damages without proving reliance on the misrepresentation but are not entitled to rescission. This is known as 'secondary market liability'. The persons signing the prospectus for the issuer and each director of the issuer at the time the prospectus was filed can be held jointly and severally liable with the issuer for a misrepresentation, though these individuals may have a due diligence defence available to them.

[56] National Instrument 45-106 *Prospectus Exemptions* ('NI 45-106') sets out a number of exemptions from the prospectus requirement, including the exemption that permits 'accredited investors' to acquire securities, which, unlike certain other exemptions available under NI 45-106, operates almost uniformly across the country. The definition of 'accredited investor' includes:

- an individual who, alone or together with a spouse, owns financial assets (which includes items such as cash and securities, but excludes a person's home) worth more than CAD1 m before taxes but net of any related liabilities;
- an individual, who alone or together with a spouse, has net assets (including real property) of at least CAD5 m;
- an individual whose net income before taxes exceeded CAD200 000 in each of the last two years and who expects to maintain at least the same level of income in the current year;
- an individual whose net income before taxes, combined with that of a spouse, exceeded CAD300 000 in each of the last two years and who expects to maintain at least the same level of income in the current year; and
- companies and certain other entities with net assets of at least CAD5 m.

[57] Three additional commonly encountered prospectus exemptions are the private issuer exemption, the 'family, friends and business associates' (FFBA) exemption and the offering memorandum exemption. The private issuer exemption permits a private issuer that meets certain requirements to distribute securities to directors, officers, employees, founders or control persons of the company and certain of their relatives, close personal friends and close business associates. The FFBA exemption allows issuers who might not qualify for the private issuer exemption to sell securities to close FFBA, though securities sold under the FFBA exemption are subject to more stringent resale requirements. The offering memorandum exemption allows issuers to sell securities up to certain dollar amounts that vary among the provinces, subject to the delivery to purchasers of a comprehensive disclosure document known as an offering memorandum.

[58] In November 2022, the listed issuer financing exemption (LIFE) was added to NI 45-106, which, provided certain requirements are met, allows issuers with equity securities listed on a Canadian stock exchange to raise up to the greater of CAD5 m and 10% of their market capitalization (up to a maximum of CAD10 m) in a twelve-month period. A key benefit of the LIFE compared to many other prospectus exemptions available under NI 45-106 is that securities issued under a LIFE are freely trading immediately after they are issued.

[59] Securities that are distributed by way of a prospectus are freely tradable unless they form part of a 'control block'. By contrast, securities issued in reliance upon a prospectus exemption are generally subject to hold period requirements of four months or more, unless there is an available prospectus exemption pursuant to which they may be resold.

Continuous Disclosure Requirements

[60] To protect the integrity of the capital markets, Canadian securities laws impose continuous disclosure obligations on reporting issuers to promote timely, fair and equal access to material information. Reporting issuers (which are typically those corporations that have filed a prospectus or whose shares are listed on a stock exchange) must periodically disclose up-to-date financial information and promptly disclose all 'material changes'. In addition, the rules of a securities exchange, such as the Toronto Stock Exchange (TSX), require prompt disclosure of the broader category of 'material information'.

Material Changes and Material Facts

[61] The identification of material changes is not always straightforward. In Ontario, the *Securities Act* defines 'material change' (for issuers other than investment funds) as follows:

- a change in the business, operations or capital of the issuer that would reasonably be expected to have a significant effect on the market price or value of any of the securities of the issuer; or
- a decision to implement such a change made by the board of directors of the issuer or other person acting in a similar capacity or by senior management of the issuer who believes that confirmation of the decision by the board of directors or such other persons acting in a similar capacity is probable.

[62] The term 'material fact', when used in relation to securities, means 'a fact that would reasonably be expected to have a significant effect on the market price or value of the securities'.

[63] Examples of material information, which includes both material changes and material facts, may include, but are not limited to:

- takeover bids, issuer bids or insider bids whether commenced or received by the issuer;
- significant reorganizations, amalgamations or mergers;
- significant acquisitions or dispositions;
- the public or private offering of additional securities;
- planned repurchases or redemptions of securities;
- any share split, consolidation, share exchange or stock dividend;
- changes in the issuer's dividend payments or policies;
- modifications to the rights of security holders;
- significant increases or decreases in near-term earnings prospects;
- significant cash flow reductions, major asset write-offs or write-downs;
- major labour disputes or disputes with major contractors or suppliers;
- changes to the board of directors or executive management;

- significant discoveries by resource companies;
- significant new contracts, products, patents, or services or significant losses of contracts or business;
- the commencement of, or developments in, significant legal proceedings or regulatory matters;
- significant new or amended credit arrangements; or
- decisions to implement any of the foregoing.

[64] If a material change has occurred, securities laws provide that the reporting issuer must immediately issue and file a news release authorized by an executive officer of the reporting issuer disclosing the nature and substance of the change and file a material change report as soon as practicable, and in any event within ten days of the date on which the change occurs.

[65] As noted, stock exchange rules generally require the prompt disclosure of material information by way of news release.

Financial Statements

[66] Reporting issuers must file and send to their shareholders comparative quarterly unaudited financial statements and audited annual financial statements. Financial statements must be prepared in accordance with International Financial Reporting Standards (IFRS) or other permitted accounting standards and must be accompanied by management's discussion and analysis (MD&A) of the corporation's financial condition and operations.

Annual Information Form

[67] Reporting issuers that are also non-venture issuers, and any issuer that wishes to carry out a distribution using a 'short form prospectus', must prepare and file an annual information form (AIF). A 'non-venture' issuer is generally one that is listed on a senior exchange, such as TSX or Cboe Canada (formerly known as the Aequitas NEO Exchange (NEO)). The AIF provides material information about the reporting issuer and its business at a point in time in the context of its historical development and possible future development. It sets out, among other things, the history and description of the issuer's business, a description of the issuer's subsidiaries and industry segments, information about the directors and officers of the issuer, information about certain financial data, information about legal or regulatory actions involving the reporting issuer, a description of the risk factors for the issuer, and information regarding the market for the issuer's securities.

Multijurisdictional Disclosure System

[68] Canadian securities regulators participate in a multijurisdictional disclosure system which affords mutual recognition between securities regulators in Canada and the US. If a US corporation meets eligibility criteria, it may distribute securities in Canada in accordance with the US regulatory requirements. There are reciprocal rules applying to eligible Canadian issuers.

The specific eligibility requirements go beyond the scope of this section; however, they include minimum public float and reporting history requirements.

Proxy Solicitation

[69] Canadian corporate legislation and Canadian securities laws each regulate the solicitation of proxies by enabling legislation to facilitate the solicitation of proxies and dictating when proxy solicitation is required.

Under the CBCA, a solicitation includes a broad number of activities including:

- a request for a proxy (even if it is not accompanied by a form of proxy);
- a request to execute or to refrain from executing a proxy;
- a request to revoke a proxy; and
- sending a form of proxy or other communication to a shareholder under circumstances reasonably calculated to result in the procurement, withholding or revocation of a proxy.

[70] With some exceptions, a reporting issuer is required to solicit proxies and distribute a management information circular in connection with a shareholders' meeting.

[71] The CBCA prohibits a person from soliciting proxies without sending a proxy circular to each shareholder whose proxy is solicited, each director of the corporation and the auditor of the corporation unless the person is a dissident, in which case they are permitted to solicit proxies from not more than fifteen shareholders (two or more joint holders being counted as one shareholder) without sending a dissident circular. If the solicitation is dissident (i.e., by or on behalf of someone other than management), the information circular must also be sent to the corporation.

[72] A solicitation does not occur – and therefore no circular is required – in certain specified circumstances. This includes the public announcement of how a shareholder intends to vote, and the reasons for that intention, if made in a public speech or publication or through a public medium.

[73] The CBCA also provides an exception to the circular requirement for a dissident solicitation made via a public broadcast, speech or publication if the solicitation sets out certain information including the name of the person making the solicitation (or on whose behalf it is made), what that person's interest is in certain transactions, and who is paying for the solicitation.

[74] The CBCA provides that the management proxy circular must be in the form provided for in Form 51-102F5 of National Instrument 51-102 *Continuous Disclosure Obligations*, together with certain additional information set out in the CBCA regulations.

[75] Although typically only registered shareholders are entitled to vote under Canadian corporate law, most Canadian public shareholders do not own their shares in registered form. Therefore, National Instrument 54-101 *Communication with Beneficial Owners of Securities of a Reporting Issuer* requires the sending of proxy materials to beneficial owners by the reporting issuer or by the intermediaries who hold the shares on behalf of their clients. A 'notice-and-access' process is in place which permits the sending of a notice of basic information about the meeting and an explanation of where to access the full proxy-related materials. The full meeting materials must be available on a website (in addition to the one maintained by the CSA).

[76] Under the notice-and-access process, the issuer must set a record date for its shareholder meeting no fewer than forty days prior to the meeting. The issuer must send a notice to all registered and beneficial owners by prepaid mail, courier or equivalent, or by email (provided that, the recipient has provided prior express consent) along with a voting instruction form or form of proxy. The notice must be sent at least thirty days before the date of the meeting. Public access must be provided to the information circular and the notice on or before the date the notice is sent. Public access is provided by posting the materials on the issuer's own website (most commonly) or a service provider's website. The issuer must also provide a toll-free number for securities holders to request a paper copy of the meeting materials.

Insider Reporting and Early Warning Reports

[77] Certain insiders (referred to as 'reporting insiders') of reporting issuers are required to report trades in and holdings of the securities of those issuers. Reporting insiders include, among others:

- directors of a reporting issuer or of a significant shareholder or major subsidiary of a reporting issuer;
- the chief executive officer, chief financial officer or chief operating officer of a reporting issuer, or of a significant shareholder or a major subsidiary of a reporting issuer;
- a person or company responsible for a principal business unit, division or function of a reporting issuer; and
- any person or company who beneficially owns, or exercises control or direction over, more than 10% of the voting rights attached to the outstanding securities of a reporting issuer.

[78] Reporting insiders must make an initial report disclosing any interests in securities of the insider that they beneficially own, control or have direction over within ten days of becoming a reporting insider. Any subsequent changes in ownership must be filed within five days.

[79] Canadian securities laws also contain an 'early warning' disclosure requirement that requires purchasers to issue and file a news release immediately and to file a report within two business days if they acquire ownership of, direction or control over, or securities convertible into, voting or equity securities of any class of a reporting issuer that constitute 10% or more of the outstanding securities of that class, either alone or in combination with other securities of the class in question already held by the purchaser. Further news releases and reports must be filed after each subsequent acquisition or disposition of 2% or more of the class. Shareholders are also required to disclose when their overall ownership, control or direction falls below 10%, which is often referred to as an 'exit report'. Early warning reporting is discussed in greater detail in paragraph 311 below.

2.1.6 Branch Operations

[80] A foreign company may carry on business through an unincorporated branch as an alternative to organizing a separate legal entity for conducting business in Canada. The question of whether any particular activity or group of activities will constitute 'carrying on business' is not specifically defined in most cases, and is to be determined by reference to the particular facts and circumstances. The foreign company must file a business name registration in all provinces in which it wishes to do business (other than Newfoundland). The registration in any particular province will be subject to the acceptability of the name of the corporation. Registration will be denied if such name is the same as, or closely resembles, the name of another corporation already incorporated or registered in the province. However, a corporation with an unacceptable corporate name may sometimes be registered to carry on business in a province under a different business name or style that is acceptable, without having to change its corporate name. In Québec, foreign corporations are also required to adopt a French trade name in conformity with the Charter of the French Language. It may also be necessary for the company, if incorporated, to register under extra-provincial corporations' legislation. The fee payable for registration of an extra-provincial licence is generally similar to that payable in respect of incorporation.

2.1.7 Management Structure

[81] The board of directors is the body of individuals empowered to manage or supervise the management of the business and affairs of the corporation, subject only to any restrictions in the articles, the by-laws, any unanimous shareholders agreement (discussed below), or the governing statute. Individual directors or committees of directors have no power to act alone unless that authority has been delegated by the board in compliance with the by-laws of the corporation, any unanimous shareholders agreement and any restrictions in the CBCA. Decisions are made at meetings of the board by way of director resolutions subject to the quorum requirements set forth in the by-laws. Typically the by-laws of the corporation will also permit decisions to be made by way of telephonic (or, more recently, virtual) meetings or by a unanimous written resolution without the necessity of calling a meeting. Directors exercise executive authority through these resolutions.

[82] Directors may (and typically do) delegate significant authority to committees of the board and to officers of the corporation, who are responsible for the day-to-day operations and affairs of the corporation. Delegation does not diminish or restrict the power of the board. The board must always have the authority to revoke the delegation of authority. There are certain non-delegable powers. These include the power to:

- submit to the shareholders any question or matter requiring the approval of the shareholders;
- fill a vacancy among the directors or in the office of the auditor, or appoint additional directors;

- issue securities except as authorized by the directors;
- declare dividends;
- purchase, redeem or otherwise acquire shares issued by the corporation;
- approve a management proxy circular;
- approve a takeover bid circular or director's circular in response to a takeover bid;
- approve any financial statements; or
- adopt, amend or repeal by-laws.

[83] Unless the articles or by-laws of or a unanimous shareholder agreement relating to a corporation otherwise provide, the directors of a corporation are empowered to cause the corporation to borrow and give security and provide a guarantee (including a guarantee of a parent company or affiliate debt). These powers may be delegated by the directors to a director, a committee of directors or to an officer of the corporation.

Size and Composition of the Board

[84] There is no limit on the size of a board of directors as long as the statutory minimum requirements are met. Private corporations must have at least one director and publicly traded corporations must have at least three directors. Typically the articles of a corporation will permit a board of variable size. Unless the by-laws of the corporation or a special resolution of the shareholders permits the board of directors to adjust the size of the board within the minimum and maximum size set out in the articles, the shareholders must fix the size of the board of directors for the following year at each annual meeting. Although infrequently used for business corporations, it is generally possible to have a staggered board. However, due to recent amendments to the CBCA, which came into force on 31 August 2022, shareholders of distributing corporations (generally, listed issuers) governed by the CBCA are to elect directors to hold office for a term ending not later than the close of the next annual meeting of shareholders following the election, thereby precluding the possibility of a staggered board for distributing corporations. It is also possible to have different classes of shareholders entitled to different voting rights in respect of the election of the board. This goes beyond the scope of this chapter. Since 1 January 2020, distributing corporations are now required to provide shareholders with information about the corporation's diversity policies at the board and senior management levels. While this requirement does not impose any quotas or specific diversity requirements, it does introduce a 'comply or explain' regime. That is, corporations are obligated to disclose the number and proportion of directors and executive officers who are members of a designated group. Corporations will also need to disclose whether they have adopted diversity policies or quotas and, if not, why.

Qualifications

[85] Certain persons are disqualified from being a director:

- anyone who is less than 18 years of age;
- anyone who is of unsound mind and has been so found by a court in Canada or elsewhere;

- a person who is not an individual (e.g., another corporation); or
- a person who has the status of bankrupt.

[86] Directors need not hold any shares of the corporation. As mentioned above, at least 25% of the directors of a CBCA corporation must be Canadian residents, or, if there are four or fewer directors, at least one must be a Canadian resident.

Appointment or Election

[87] The first directors are appointed by operation of law upon the filing of the articles of incorporation setting out the first directors and the issuance of the certificate of incorporation. Subsequently, directors are elected by the shareholders at annual meetings.

[88] It is also possible for directors to be appointed by the board of directors to fill a casual vacancy. This technique is frequently employed in the context of mergers and acquisitions. A director on the incumbent board will resign with the remaining board appointing a replacement from the acquirer's slate. The process will then be repeated seriatim until all or the agreed-upon number of directors have been replaced. Directors appointed in this way will hold their positions until the next annual meeting unless the board is made up of directors with staggered terms. In the case of staggered terms, a director who is appointed this way will hold office for the balance of the resigning director's term.

[89] A person may also be a director because of an office that the director holds (an ex officio director). Ex officio directors may or may not vote depending on the by-laws of the corporation. A person may not be elected or appointed to a board of directors without his or her permission.

[90] As noted above, directors need not all hold the same term of office. Therefore, except for distributing corporations governed by the CBCA, it is possible to have staggered boards in which only a portion of the directors are elected to office each year. In the absence of a specified term, the term shall be until the close of the next annual meeting after the director's election or appointment.

Fiduciary Duties

[91] Directors have a fiduciary duty to act honestly, in good faith and with a view to the best interests of the corporation, and must also exercise the care, diligence and skill that a reasonable and prudent person would exercise in comparable circumstances.

Resignation and Removal

[92] The Ontario *Business Corporations Act* provides that the first directors of the corporation may not resign unless a successor is elected or appointed. Thereafter, directors may resign at any time. There is no equivalent in the CBCA, which permits directors to resign at any time. Resignations are effective at the time the written resignation is sent to the corporation or the time specified in the resignation.

[93] Directors may cease to be directors by operation of law. A director ceases to hold office upon death or if disqualified from eligibility (discussed above). A director also ceases to hold office upon being removed by an ordinary resolution of shareholders at a special meeting of shareholders called for that purpose.

2.1.8 Partnerships

[94] There is no federal law governing partnerships. Instead, partnerships are governed by provincial law. There are three types of partnerships recognized provincially – general partnerships, limited partnerships and limited liability partnerships. Limited liability partnerships are typically restricted to professional services firms, such as law firms and accounting firms, and will not be discussed here.

[95] All forms of partnership involve a relationship between two or more persons carrying on business in common (which can be in the nature of an ongoing business or a specific transaction) with a view to profit (which excludes charitable and cultural organizations). Partners may be individuals (natural persons), corporations, or, in some cases, other partnerships.

General Partnerships

[96] The law of general partnerships (also known as ordinary partnerships) is relatively uniform across all provinces. The law in the common law provinces (all provinces except Québec) is ultimately based on the 1890 UK *Partnerships Act*. Although Québec has its own civil law form of partnership, its characteristics are substantially the same as those of the common law provinces.

[97] As a vehicle for conducting business, the most advantageous characteristics of a partnership are the ability to allocate and flow losses through to the partners and to adjust the allocation of profits between partners as part of tax planning strategies.

[98] There are five fundamental characteristics of general partnerships:

(1) the partnership is not a juridical person (except where provided for by statute, such as for the computation of partnership income for tax purposes);
(2) partners have unlimited liability for the liabilities and losses of the partnership;
(3) mutual agency of partners (each partner is the agent of the other partner and may bind the partnership unless there are restrictions in the partnership agreement of which the third party has notice);
(4) each partner is a fiduciary of the other; and
(5) partners do not have a direct interest in the partnership assets (any assets held by a partner are held in trust for the benefit of the partnership).

[99] Beyond these characteristics, a partnership is a flexible structure permitting wide variation in terms of organization. Although it is unnecessary to enter into a formal partnership agreement in order to organize a partnership, a formal, written agreement is desirable. In the absence of an agreement on certain issues, provincial partnership legislation will provide default rules. The default rules that parties entering into a partnership will wish to address include the following:

- equality of interest in the capital and profits of the partnership;
- mutual indemnification of partners in respect of costs incurred in the partnership;
- equal right to participate in the management of the partnership business;
- decisions may be decided by a majority vote of the partners;
- admission of a new partner requires unanimous consent;
- change to the nature of the business requires unanimous consent;
- each partner may inspect books and records of the partnership;
- partnership can be dissolved by a single partner; and
- the partnership automatically dissolves on the death or bankruptcy of a partner.

As noted above, each of these default rules can be (and typically are) varied in the partnership agreement.

[100] In a general partnership, each partner is jointly liable with the other partners to the full extent of the partner's personal assets. The estate of a deceased partner remains liable for partnership debts incurred when the partner was alive. However, a partner can be discharged from a partnership by an agreement and will not thereafter be responsible for debts incurred after the signing of such an agreement.

Limited Partnerships

[101] Limited partnerships are an alternative to the general partnership structure. Like general partnerships, limited partnerships permit the allocation and flow through of losses to the partners and provide for a flexible structure within which to allocate partnership profits. This form of partnership is used primarily for financing where passive investors are involved, and it is desirable for profits and losses to flow through to the investors. It is also used by investors that are non-taxable entities, such as government-related agencies (e.g., some public utilities or provincial development agencies), where the investor wishes to avoid holding its investment in a company that is required to pay taxes before distributing its income to its shareholders. However, unlike a general partnership, not all partners will be liable for the losses and liabilities of the partnership.

[102] Limited partnerships have two classes of partners: one or more general partners and one or more limited partners. The general partner manages the partnership and holds title to real property. Typically it is a special purpose corporation that only holds assets related to the partnership business. A limited partner has a participatory interest in the profits and assets of the partnership business but is not involved in the management of the partnership. Generally, the interest of a limited partner is assignable if all the partners consent to the assignment or if the partnership agreement permits it.

[103] A limited partner's potential liability is limited to the investment in the limited partnership. Accordingly, a limited partner is similar to a shareholder in a corporation with limited shareholder liability. A general partner may also be a limited partner. However, in all provinces other than Manitoba a limited partner who takes part in the management of the business will lose the benefit of limited liability.

[104] General partners in a limited partnership have the same rights and obligations as in general partnerships, except that certain actions of the general partner may require the prior consent of the limited partners. It is common to have a corporation as the general partner because of the limited liability feature of the corporation.

[105] In Manitoba, a limited partner will not lose the benefit of limited partnership unless the limited partner takes part in the management of the business of the partnership and the following two criteria are satisfied: (1) the limited partner deals with the third party on behalf of the partnership; and (2) the third party does not know that the limited partner is a limited partner.

2.1.9 Joint Ventures

[106] Joint ventures are frequently employed in natural resource development in Canada. The term 'joint venture' is used to describe the combination of resources by two or more persons in order to conduct a commercial venture under agreed-upon rules. A joint venture may take the form of a partnership, a co-ownership of property or a corporation. Generally, the parties to a joint venture will enter into a written agreement (whether a partnership agreement, a co-ownership agreement or a shareholders' agreement), which establishes the respective rights and obligations of the parties in respect of the venture.

[107] Typically the purpose of forming a joint venture will be to obtain the advantages of a partnership without the imposition of fiduciary obligations upon the partners and the potential for unlimited joint and several liability with respect to the activities of the partnership business. To avoid being found to be a partnership, the joint venture may be structured for a single purpose, of specific duration, expressly not a partnership, and with specific rules regarding how liabilities may be incurred and to whose account.

[108] Whether an arrangement is a joint venture or a partnership may have important legal consequences, including tax consequences. Even though the income of a partnership is taxed in the hands of the partners after allocation, it is calculated as if the partnership were a distinct entity. Therefore, a partnership deducts expenses and capital cost allowances from its income before the allocation of profits. By contrast, revenue and expenses of a joint venture are allocated to each participant in the joint venture. Net taxable income is determined by each participant in combination with all other income and expenses.

[109] A partnership interest is usually treated as capital property for income tax purposes. If a partnership interest is sold, it may result in a capital gain or loss. However, a joint venture interest is not recognized as capital property. Instead, each asset sold may result in a capital gain or loss. Upon the dissolution of a partnership, there is usually a disposition of property. However, no such disposition occurs in the joint venture unless there is also a change in ownership.

[110] There is no prevailing statutory definition for a joint venture. Courts and taxation authorities will examine a number of factors including the intentions of the parties as determined by a written agreement or their conduct. The factors that will be relevant are:

- whether the parties treated the property as their common property (i.e., partnership property) or whether each participant maintains ownership of any property contributed to the joint venture;
- whether the arrangement involves specifying percentage interests in the products produced by the joint venture as opposed to specifying percentage interests in the profits of the business;
- whether the business is limited to a specific undertaking, such as to construct a building and to lease space in it;
- whether the participants are all involved in the daily operation of the business (which is usually not a feature of a joint venture, where one of the parties may be the manager);
- whether the participants are liable solely for their own expenses or a proportion of expenses and whether there is a prohibition on the participants incurring obligations for one another.

2.2 Laws Affecting M&A

[111] There are a number of ways to acquire a public company under Canadian law. These include:

- a plan of arrangement in which cash, shares or other property is exchanged for the shares of the target;
- a takeover bid under securities laws;
- an asset purchase from the target; and
- a statutory amalgamation of the target with a subsidiary of the acquirer.

[112] The plan of arrangement is the most frequently used method to acquire a public company and is discussed in detail here. The plan of arrangement is typically deployed only in 'friendly' transactions as it requires the cooperation of the target company's board of directors. A takeover bid is more typical where the acquisition is 'hostile' and is discussed later in this section.

2.2.1 Plan of Arrangement Transactions

[113] A plan of arrangement, also known as an 'arrangement' or 'statutory arrangement', is the most common method by which Canadian public companies are acquired – in fact, nearly 100% of negotiated transactions are completed by way of an arrangement. There are four key features of the plan of arrangement process that distinguish it from a takeover bid process, which is often used in a more hostile or unfriendly manner. First, the plan of arrangement is governed by a corporate statute, such as the CBCA or a provincial or territorial corporations act whereas a takeover bid is governed by national and provincial securities instruments. Second, a plan of arrangement requires that a court approve the fairness of the transaction. Third, a plan of arrangement is a transaction that requires approval from the board of directors of the target company whereas a takeover bid is made directly by the bidder to the shareholders of the target company (it is worth noting that in negotiated takeover bids, which very rarely occur, the target board would approve the entering into of the definitive agreement with the bidder). Fourth, if approved, the plan of arrangement is binding on all shareholders of the target company, such that 100% of the target is acquired in one step whereas a takeover bid is typically a two-step transaction.

[114] A statutory arrangement can be used for a variety of purposes not related to public mergers and acquisitions, including, in respect of insolvency proceedings. The term 'plan of arrangement' has become synonymous with arrangements that involve a public acquisition transaction. The term technically refers to – and originated from – the document that sets out the steps in the transaction. The actual plan of arrangement is typically attached to the arrangement agreement which is the key definitive agreement among the applicable parties that governs the transaction. This section primarily refers to the term plan of arrangement as the overall transaction or process.

[115] The plan of arrangement process requires two court appearances. The first is for an 'Interim Order' to facilitate the calling, holding and voting on the transaction(s) at a meeting of the security holders of the target company whose rights are being 'arranged'. Although some corporate statutes do not explicitly require a security holder vote, the court treats these votes as a critical part of the process. At the interim order, the court is mostly focused on the process of the upcoming meeting and deals with the fairness of the transaction at the second appearance. Provided that the affirmative vote of two-thirds of the security holders present in person or by proxy is obtained at the security holders' meeting, a second court appearance is held for a 'Final Order' approving the arrangement. At the final hearing, the court will consider the fairness of the transaction. The requirements for approval are discussed in the paragraphs below.

[116] A plan of arrangement is attractive for a number of reasons. First, it allows for tax planning as the steps in the plan of arrangement can be set out in a particular order, however, none is effective unless all are effective. Second, as a plan of arrangement results in the acquisition of 100% of the target on closing, it may be easier for an acquirer to obtain financing under a plan of arrangement.

[117] Another advantage to a plan of arrangement is that it assists in dealing with stock options and employees' incentive plans that do not have termination or accelerated vesting in change-of-control transactions. Finally, if the consideration for the acquisition includes shares of the acquirer, there is an exemption from the U.S. registration requirements for shares issued to U.S. shareholders referred to as the '3(a)(10)' exemption – named simply after the section of the US Securities Act of 1933 that provides the exemption – as discussed in more detail below.

Types of Arrangements

[118] In a takeover or merger context, the plan of arrangement is most commonly used to facilitate a share exchange type transaction. A commonly used structure is the 'three-cornered' transaction, involving the following core steps:

- the acquirer will incorporate a wholly owned subsidiary for the purposes of the acquisition (Acquisition Co);
- the acquirer may loan Acquisition Co the funds necessary to complete the transaction;
- Acquisition Co will then exchange cash, shares in the acquirer or both for the shares held by the target company's shareholders;
- as a result of the share exchange, the shareholders of the target company become shareholders of the acquirer and/or receive cash;
- the target company becomes the wholly owned subsidiary of Acquisition Co; and
- Acquisition Co and the target company amalgamate.

[119] When the transaction involves a foreign acquirer that is using its shares as consideration, the plan of arrangement will sometimes include an exchangeable share structure. This structure enables Canadian resident shareholders to exchange their shares for Acquisition Co shares that are exchangeable at the holder's option for shares in the foreign acquirer. Since target and Acquisition Co are both Canadian companies, this structure generally permits Canadian resident shareholders of the target to take advantage of a tax-deferred rollover with respect to the exchange of their shares. The shareholder may defer any capital gains until it sells the exchangeable shares or exercises the exchange right. Normally, however, the exchangeable shares will be subject to a forced exchange after a certain period of time. When using this structure, the exchangeable shares will have a right to receive dividends that are the same as and payable at the same time as the purchaser's common shares. There will be an equivalent right to vote at shareholder meetings and to participate equivalently in a dissolution. This structure can be expensive and cumbersome, so it will not be appropriate in all transactions.

[120] A plan of arrangement may also amend a company's equity compensation plans. In all cash transactions, equity awards of target are generally cashed out on closing, based on the exercise price of the underlying award with out-of-the-money awards usually cancelled without any compensation. In transactions where the consideration includes shares of the acquirer, particularly where the shares are publicly traded, the target company's outstanding equity awards will be replaced with new awards exercisable into the acquirer's shares. It is also possible to spin out assets into other companies as steps in the plan of arrangement, the shares of which may be issued either to the existing shareholders of the target or a separate purchaser. Changes to equity compensation awards that are not permitted by the underlying equity compensation plan cause the plan of arrangement to be subject to approval of such equity award holders, so care must be taken in this regard.

U.S. Securities Act, 1933 Exemption

[121] The plan of arrangement process substantially simplifies the process in a share exchange type acquisition or merger for companies with shareholders in the US. Section 3(a)(10) of the US *Securities Act of 1933* (the '1933 Act') exempts securities from the registration requirement for the issuance of securities if (a) the issuance has been approved by a court of competent jurisdiction after a hearing on the fairness of the terms and conditions of issuance and (b) all holders of the target's securities receive notice of the hearing and have an opportunity to attend and be heard. The US Securities and Exchange Commission (SEC) has expressly recognized the Canadian plan of arrangement process as satisfying the requirements of section 3(a)(10) of the 1933 Act.

[122] The plan of arrangement process therefore provides a significant benefit where the Canadian target company has a significant number of US shareholders because it enables the acquirer to issue its shares to the shareholders of the target in a share exchange transaction without any SEC review. The plan of arrangement process is also advantageous to a US acquirer of a Canadian target. If a US acquirer's shareholders are not required to vote on the transaction then the SEC proxy rules will not apply. Since Canadian foreign private issuers are exempt from the SEC proxy rules, the plan of arrangement simplifies the acquisition process.

Statutory Requirements

[123] There are three statutory requirements for a plan of arrangement under the CBCA: (1) the structure must involve an 'arrangement' (i.e., a transaction); (2) the company proposing the plan of arrangement (the 'applicant') must not be 'insolvent'; and (3) the proposed transaction must be impracticable under any other provision of the CBCA.

What qualifies as an 'arrangement' is open-ended. It includes, among other things:

- an amendment to the articles of a corporation;
- the amalgamation of two or more corporations;
- a division of the business carried on by a corporation;
- the reorganization of a company's share structure;
- an exchange of securities of one corporation for property, money or securities of another corporation;
- a transfer of all or substantially all of the property of one corporation for property, money or securities of another corporation;
- a liquidation and dissolution of a corporation;
- a going-private transaction or a squeeze-out transaction; and
- any combination of the foregoing.

[124] In the case of CBCA corporations, the second statutory requirement is that the target company not be insolvent. A company is insolvent for this purpose if (a) it is unable to pay its liabilities as they become due, or (b) the realizable value of the assets of the company is less than the aggregate of its liabilities and stated capital of all classes. The value of a company's assets may be different for the purposes of the solvency test than in the company's financial statements. Asset values are normally to be assessed on the basis of the assets or the company being sold as a going concern. Courts have held that only one of the applicants in a plan of arrangement needs to be solvent, thereby permitting structures to satisfy the CBCA requirements even though the main target company is insolvent. For example, a co-applicant to the plan of arrangement could be a solvent wholly owned subsidiary of the target company.

[125] The final statutory requirement under the CBCA is that it is impracticable to effect the transaction being proposed by the applicant under any other provision of the CBCA. In a Policy Statement, the Director appointed under the CBCA endorses the view that the test for impracticability 'would be satisfied by demonstrating that it would be inconvenient or less advantageous to the corporation to proceed under other provisions' of the CBCA, provided that the plan of arrangement process is not being used to 'subvert the procedural or substantive safeguards' applicable to other types of transactions permitted under the CBCA.

Procedural Steps

[126] Procedurally, there are six main steps to the plan of arrangement process. Because the plan of arrangement requires the support and sponsorship of the board of directors of the target company, the first step is to negotiate a definitive 'arrangement agreement' with the target company, which defines the terms of the transaction, the steps in the plan of arrangement, and any representations, warranties and covenants, including any support provisions.

[127] A key and highly negotiated set of provisions in the arrangement agreement are the 'non-solicit' or 'fiduciary out' clauses. These clauses generally preclude the target company from soliciting or dealing with any other offers to acquire the company after the arrangement agreement has been signed subject to a few common exceptions.

[128] The most common exception allows the target to discuss and negotiate a transaction with a third party that has made an unsolicited proposal that meets certain requirements, most notably that it is a 'superior proposal' (all as negotiated and set out in the arrangement agreement). In most cases (which remain subject to negotiation), a target will only be permitted to enter into a definitive agreement with a third party and terminate the agreement with the acquirer, if among other things, the initial acquirer has had an opportunity to match the superior proposal and if it does not do so, it is paid a break fee.

[129] The next step in the plan of arrangement process is for the target company to apply to the court for an 'Interim Order'. This sets the approval process 'in motion' and establishes the parameters for the holding of the security holders meeting to consider the arrangement. The contents of the Initial Order and the issues that must be decided by the target company prior to applying for the Initial Order are discussed below in detail.

[130] The third step is for the target to prepare and deliver a Notice of Meeting, an Information Circular and a form of proxy, in connection with the security holders meeting to its shareholders and certain other security holders. These documents are also discussed in detail below.

[131] The fourth step is for the target to hold a meeting of security holders. In some cases, it will also be necessary under the rules of the relevant stock exchange for the acquirer to hold a meeting of its shareholders to vote on the issuance of shares in connection with a share exchange type of arrangement.

[132] The fifth step is to return to the court following the security holders' meeting to report on the outcome of the shareholders' vote, and to seek a 'Final Order' approving the plan of arrangement.

[133] The final step is to close or consummate the transactions provided for in the plan of arrangement and to file Articles of Arrangement.

Initial Order

[134] Once the arrangement agreement is entered into by the acquirer and the target company, the target company will commence a proceeding in court for approval of the plan of arrangement and bring a motion for an Interim Order. The Interim Order will generally address the following matters:

- setting the record date for the meeting of shareholders and, if applicable, other security holders;
- approving the date, time and place for the meeting;
- setting quorum requirements;
- approving the form of proxy to be used and specifying a proxy 'cut-off' date;
- permitting the acquirer to solicit proxies on behalf of the target company;
- approving the form of notice and circular to be sent to shareholders and other security holders whose interests may be affected whether or not they are permitted to vote;
- approving class voting requirements, if applicable;
- setting the levels of approval from each class of security holder who is voting, including any requirements for approval by a 'majority of the minority';
- providing for and usually modifying dissent rights for security holders;
- setting out who may attend the meeting of security holders; and
- providing for the requirements for notice and specifying who may appear in connection with the final hearing to approve the arrangement.

Security Holders' Vote

[135] Although the CBCA does not require that shareholders vote on the plan of arrangement, the court will ordinarily require shareholder approval. Provincial statutes typically require a shareholder vote. The threshold for approval may vary among provinces depending on whether the arrangement involves shareholders only or also includes creditors. Typically shareholder approval requires the affirmative vote of 66 2/3% of the votes cast at the shareholders meeting.

[136] In general, all security holders whose legal rights are being arranged are entitled to vote on the plan of arrangement. In addition, security holders of a particular class whose legal rights are not being arranged (such as holders of debt securities) may be entitled to vote if the plan of arrangement fundamentally alters the nature of their investment. However, absent special considerations, the indenture, contract or other document creating the security will usually be determinative as to whether the security holder is entitled to vote. Moreover, the mere fact that the security holders may face a reduction in the trading value of their securities will not be sufficient to require a vote.

[137] For purposes of the vote, the target company's security holders may be grouped into classes. For example, the Initial Order could provide that all common shareholders and preferred shareholders will vote in a single class. If option holders, debt holders or other stakeholders' legal rights are being arranged, then the order might provide for those stakeholders to vote in a single class along with shareholders or they might be grouped in some other manner. The classification or grouping of stakeholders whose legal rights are being arranged is to be made according to commonality of interest. It is not necessary that the stakeholders who are being permitted to vote have an identity of interest. It is only necessary that their interests are sufficiently similar so that they may consult together towards a common interest. The company may not, therefore, manipulate the vote by putting stakeholders with countervailing interests together in order to dilute the outcome.

[138] In some cases, it will be necessary to obtain 'majority of the minority' support in order to comply with the requirements for approval of non-arm's length, related party or going-private transactions. This requirement is imposed by applicable securities laws (such as Multilateral Instrument 61-101 *Protection of Minority Security Holders in Special Transactions*) and the rules of relevant Canadian stock exchanges. In order to obtain approval under these provisions, it is necessary that a simple majority of those persons who do not have any 'collateral interest' in the transaction vote in favour. For example, if the acquirer already holds shares in the target company, it may be necessary to determine whether the transaction was approved by a majority of shares cast excluding the votes of the acquirer. Similarly, if a portion of the assets of the target company is going to be spun out to the management of the target company as part of a separate management buyout, it will be necessary to determine whether a majority of shares voted, not including those of management, were cast in favour of the plan of arrangement.

Dissent Rights

[139] The provisions of the CBCA and provincial statutes do not in all cases require that dissent rights be provided to shareholders whose legal rights are being arranged in a plan of arrangement. However, the court (and, in the case of a CBCA corporation, the CBCA Director) will require that dissent rights be provided in the Initial Order unless there are clear reasons not to do so. It is only in exceptional cases, therefore, that it is possible to dispense with dissent rights for a class of security holders whose rights are being affected.

[140] The Interim Order usually modifies dissent rights for shareholders. In particular, the timing for dissent is usually accelerated modestly to require shareholders to register their dissent a few days prior to the meeting of security holders. In addition, the Initial Order usually provides that once a shareholder registers a dissent, the shareholder ceases to be a shareholder of the company for all purposes and only has a debt claim for the fair value of those shares. This ensures that the acquirer company can complete the plan of arrangement and acquire all of the issued and outstanding shares, irrespective of any outstanding rights of the dissenting shareholders.

Purchaser's Shareholder Vote

[141] If the consideration for the purchase of the target company's securities will involve securities of the purchaser, it might be necessary for the shareholders of the purchaser to vote on the issuance of shares that are to be exchanged as consideration. If the securities to be issued exceed 25% of the listed issuer's outstanding securities, the TSX Rules require that the purchaser's shareholders approve the issuance of shares in connection with the transaction.

Fairness Opinion

[142] Typically, the board of directors of the target company will retain an independent financial advisor to deliver a 'fairness opinion' with respect to the plan of arrangement. The financial advisor evaluates whether the transaction is fair from a financial point of view to the affected security holders. Although this practice is not a requirement under the CBCA or other statutes in Canada, it has been strongly endorsed by the CBCA Director. Unless it can be demonstrated that the plan of arrangement is inherently fair to the affected security holders, the court will expect that a fairness opinion will be part of the meeting material delivered to the shareholders.

[143] Best practice dictates that this 'fairness advisor' be compensated on a fixed-fee basis, i.e., its fee should not be contingent on the conclusion reached or the outcome of the transaction. A success-based fee payable to the advisor could taint the transaction such that court approval is not granted, irrespective of the outcome of the security holder's vote. As many financial advisors do receive a success-based fee, it is fairly common in Canada for a target company to get two fairness opinions – one from its financial advisor and a second one that is delivered to the board, and/or a special committee of the board from an independent financial advisor that will not receive a success-based fee, but rather just a fee for rendering its fairness opinion regardless of the outcome of the transaction.

Disclosure

[144] For reporting issuers in Canada, a press release and material change report are generally issued at the time that the arrangement agreement is executed. It is possible that a material change could occur prior to entering into the arrangement agreement, however, parties are usually careful to be sure that there is enough uncertainty around a transaction to avoid premature disclosure.

[145] In anticipation of the meeting of affected security holders, the target company will usually begin drafting a 'management information circular' upon execution of, or in some cases contemporaneously with negotiating, the arrangement agreement. The circular is the main document by which the company will describe the terms of and background to the plan of arrangement, and solicit proxies in favour of the resolution approving the plan of arrangement.

[146] The circular must contain sufficient information to permit a reasonable security holder to form a reasoned judgment concerning the nature and effect of the plan of arrangement on the target company and the resulting entity or entities. In a share exchange transaction, for example, the circular must provide financial disclosure with respect to the acquirer and the expected financial position of the combined entity. The circular must also contain governance-related disclosure regarding the acquirer and the expected governance practices of the combined entity, including the composition of the board of directors of the combined entity.

[147] The circular will ordinarily describe the genesis of the transaction and the events leading up to the approval by the board of directors of the target company. It will describe the factors that the board of directors took into account in approving the arrangement. Usually, the circular will also contain a recommendation to the security holders to vote in favour of the arrangement resolution approving the plan of arrangement and a detailed section disclosing the reasons why the plan of arrangement is in the interests of the security holders.

[148] The fairness opinion, will be disclosed and appended to the circular, along with the plan of arrangement, the arrangement agreement and the Interim Order. The target company must also disclose whether the provider of the fairness opinion has any relationship with a party involved in the plan of arrangement, as well as whether the provider's compensation is in any way contingent on a successful vote or the consummation of the transactions in the plan of arrangement. As noted, any perceived lack of independence of the financial advisor or disclosure failure in this respect could preclude final court approval. If the consideration for the arrangement includes shares of the acquirer, detailed disclosure regarding the acquirer will be included.

Test for Final Order

[149] The court focuses on the terms and impact of the plan of arrangement when determining whether to approve it. The target company bears the onus of satisfying the court that (a) the statutory requirements have been met; (b) the application has been put forward in good faith; and (c) the plan of arrangement is fair and reasonable.

[150] The first part of the test for approval requires that the target company demonstrate that it has fulfilled the statutory requirements (discussed above) for approval of a plan of arrangement and that the target company has followed the terms of the Interim Order, including obtaining the requisite level of security holder approval.

[151] The second part of the test for approval requires that the target company demonstrate that the application has been put forward in good faith. This is generally not an onerous task. Unless the plan of arrangement is challenged on the basis that the directors are using the plan of arrangement process for an improper purpose, this requirement is usually met by demonstrating that the directors have used a sound process for negotiating and recommending a transaction that is in the best interests of the corporation. Thus, for example, steps taken by the company to minimize conflicts by forming a special committee of independent directors to evaluate and, in some cases, to negotiate the terms of the plan of arrangement will assist in demonstrating to the court that the process has been taken in good faith.

[152] The test for whether a plan of arrangement is 'fair and reasonable' is not as onerous as those words might imply. The fairness opinion and security holder vote will generally be afforded considerable weight. However, the test also requires that the target company demonstrate that (a) the arrangement has a valid business purpose and (b) the objections of any persons whose legal rights are being arranged have been resolved in a fair and balanced way.

[153] To demonstrate that the plan of arrangement has a valid business purpose, the target company must demonstrate that the proposed plan of arrangement is justified in the interests of the corporation as a going concern. There is no blueprint with respect to the factors that the court will consider. However, in general, if the plan of arrangement is necessary for the continued existence of the target company, then the court will more willingly approve the plan of arrangement despite prejudicial effects on the security holders.

[154] In assessing whether the objections of any persons whose legal rights are being arranged have been resolved in a fair and balanced way, the court will consider whether the plan of arrangement overall favours one group of security holders over others. The court will also consider the reputation of the directors and advisors who endorsed the plan of arrangement, whether a special committee of independent directors approved the plan of arrangement, whether an independent fairness opinion was obtained, and whether shareholders have dissent and appraisal remedies. In addition, the court will consider the number of security holders who voted and the outcome of that vote. The overwhelming vote of properly informed security holders whose rights are being arranged will be compelling evidence of the fairness of the plan of arrangement.

2.2.2 Amalgamations

[155] If the consideration for the acquisition of the target will involve shares of the acquirer, a 'three-cornered' amalgamation may prove to be the most tax-advantageous structure for the shareholders of the target company. In this structure, the acquirer will typically incorporate a wholly owned subsidiary under the same laws as that which govern the target company for the purpose of effecting the amalgamation. The subsidiary and the target then amalgamate in a transaction in which shareholders of the target receive shares in the acquirer.

[156] Under the amalgamation structure, the amalgamated corporation is the successor of both amalgamating corporations. It succeeds, therefore, in all of the rights, liabilities and obligations of the predecessor companies.

2.3 Relevant Regulatory Authorities

[157] In Canada, certain business transactions require regulatory approval before they can be completed.

2.3.1 Competition Bureau

[158] The Competition Bureau (the 'Bureau') administers and enforces the Competition Act. Parties to certain types of transactions that exceed prescribed financial thresholds must notify the Commissioner of Competition (the 'Commissioner'), who heads the Bureau, of the transaction. The Bureau will determine whether to challenge the transaction on the basis that it will result in the substantial lessening of or preventing competition in the market. Challenges to transactions are adjudicated in the Competition Tribunal (the 'Tribunal'). If a transaction does not require notification, it may still be challenged within a three-year period following substantial completion of the transaction – unless the parties voluntarily make a filing, in which case the limitation period is one year.

2.3.2 Securities Regulators

[159] The regulation of securities laws in Canada falls largely within provincial responsibility. There is no national regulator. Although provincial securities legislation is not identical, the basic regulatory concepts are similar. In addition, provincial regulators coordinate regulatory initiatives through the CSA, which is an umbrella organization of provincial and territorial securities administrators. The CSA has implemented a national 'passport' system in every province other than Ontario, which allows issuers and registrants to deal only with the regulator in their principal jurisdictions on most matters. In addition, the structure of Canada's market has resulted in a few of the provincial regulators dominating the policy-making process, being the Ontario Securities Commission, Alberta Securities Commission, British Columbia Securities Commission and Québec's Autorité des Marchés Financiers.

[160] Canadian securities laws do not contain an exhaustive definition of a 'security'. In Ontario, for example, the *Securities Act* defines security to include shares, bonds, debentures, any document constituting evidence of title to or interest in the capital, assets, property, profits, earnings or royalties of any person or company and, most broadly, any 'investment contract', among other things. Canadian securities laws also take an expansive approach to defining trades and distributions.

[161] In addition to complying with securities laws, a corporation or other entity that intends to list its securities on a Canadian stock exchange must comply with the additional requirements of such exchange.

Regulatory Mechanisms

[162] The overall objectives of Canadian securities legislation are to ensure a fair and efficient capital market and to protect investors. This is addressed principally through the following three mechanisms:

(1) *Registration of participants*. Participants in the capital markets who are in the business of trading in securities, underwriting securities or advising with respect to investing in securities must be registered. 'Trading in securities' includes an original issue of securities as well as secondary market activity. There are a limited number of exemptions from the registration requirements.

(2) *Qualification of securities and continuous disclosure*. There are detailed disclosure requirements both in a prospectus for an issue of securities and ongoing 'continuous disclosure' requirements.

(3) *Takeover bid/Issuer bid requirements*. There are detailed rules governing the acquisition of public companies and acquisitions by an issuer of its own securities.

2.3.3 Stock Exchanges

[163] The framework for the transfer of securities in Canada is mature and regulated by a coordinated system of provincial laws.

[164] Canada's capital markets are dominated by pension funds, mutual funds, private equity funds, banks, trust companies and life insurance companies, although individual investors are also active.

[165] There are four principal stock exchanges in Canada: (1) the TSX; (2) the TSX Venture Exchange (TSXV); (3) the NEO; and (4) the Canadian Securities Exchange (CSE). The TMX Group Inc. operates the TSX and the TSXV. The TSX is the most well-known senior equity market in Canada. The TSXV is a public exchange focusing on emerging venture capital companies. The NEO is an exchange that was acquired by Cboe Global Markets from Aequitas Innovations Inc. in 2022 and represents approximately 15% of all trading volume of Canadian listed securities. The CSE is an exchange owned and operated by CNSX Markets Inc. that offers simplified reporting requirements and reduced barriers to listing. In addition to the principal exchanges, there are other exchanges such as the Montréal Exchange (also operated by the TMX Group Inc.), which is dedicated to the development of the Canadian derivatives market. This chapter will focus on the TSX and TSXV, which are the predominant exchanges for public equity trading.

Listing Requirements

[166] The conditions for seeking to list on the TSX and TSXV are similar. In both cases, the company must complete a listing application. In the case of the TSXV, this may be a letter application. The application must reference either a prospectus, in the case of an IPO, or an annual information statement or other principal disclosure document in other cases. Companies must also provide documentation establishing that the company satisfies the listing requirements. Listing requirements vary by sector and are summarized at the end of this section for (a) mining and exploration companies and (b) technology companies.

[167] There are two levels of financial standards for listing on the TSX. 'Exempt Issuers' are companies that meet prescribed levels of pre-tax profitability and cash flow. 'Non-Exempt Issuers' have lower (or no) levels of profit and cash flow. Non-exempt Issuers must obtain advance TSX acceptance of proposed material changes and are generally subject to greater scrutiny. In general, Exempt Issuers do not have to obtain pre-acceptance of material changes except for the issuance of shares. The TSXV also maintains two levels of financial standards for listing. 'Tier 1 Issuers' are companies which have greater financial strength than 'Tier 2 Issuers'. If a listed issuer ceases to meet the financial requirements for listing on the TSXV it may continue to trade on the NEX board, also maintained by the TMX Group Inc., which is a trading forum for listed companies that have fallen below the TSXV's ongoing listing standards.

[168] With the exception of certain TSX Exempt Issuers and Non-Exempt issuers with a market capitalization greater than CAD100 m, the TSX and TSXV impose escrow requirements for equity holdings for insiders of the company. These requirements vary depending on the issuer status of the company. These requirements restrict the ability of insiders to sell securities for a period of time, which may run from six to thirty-six months after the date of the listing. It should be noted that Canadian securities laws may also impose a hold period for securities issued prior to an IPO or in connection with other transactions.

[169] Directors, officers and other insiders of an issuer seeking a listing must complete a personal information form. This requires disclosure of information relating to the identity of the director, officer or insider as well as the individual's history with reporting issuers or companies that have been denied listings in Canada and elsewhere. The personal information form also requires disclosure of certain offences that the individual has either been charged with or convicted of as well as regulatory offences. If a person has been convicted of a fraud-related offence but has been pardoned, the pardon must be disclosed. The director, officer or insider must agree to submit to the jurisdiction of the TSX or TSXV (as applicable) and to the Canadian Investment Regulatory Organization, the organization that oversees all investment dealers, mutual fund dealers and trading activity in Canada and carries on regulatory functions formerly managed by the Investment Industry Regulatory Organization of Canada. The director, officer or insider must also consent to the release of criminal record information for the purposes of conducting background checks.

[170] The following tables provide information on certain listing requirements for selected types of issuers. The tables are not comprehensive and are frequently evolving with new categories being made available to issuers. Reference should be made to the TMX listing requirements, which are available at www.tmx.com or through your legal advisor. Listing requirements for NEO and CSE are also available at www.cboe.ca and www.thecse.com, respectively.

Mining: Overview of Select Listing Requirements

Listing Requirement	*TSX Venture Tier 2 Issuers*	*TSX Venture Tier 1*	*TSX Non-exempt Exploration and Development Stage Issuers*	*TSX Non-exempt Producer Issuers*	*TSX Exempt Issuers*
Working Capital and Financial Resources	CAD100 000 in unallocated funds; adequate working capital and financial resources to carry out twelve-month plan following listing	CAD200 000 in unallocated funds; adequate working capital and financial resources to carry out eighteen-month plan following listing	CAD2 m working capital; sufficient and adequate working capital and financial resources to carry out eighteen-month plan following listing	Adequate funds to bring property into commercial production and adequate working capital for all budgeted capital expenditures and to carry on business. Appropriate capital structure	Adequate working capital to carry on the business. Appropriate capital structure
Assets, Earnings or Revenue	No requirement	CAD2 m net tangible assets	CAD3 m net tangible assets	CAD4 m net tangible assets	CAD7.5 m net tangible assets
Earnings & Revenue	No requirement	No requirement	No requirement	Reasonable likelihood of future profitability supported by a feasibility study	Pre-tax profitability from ongoing operations in last fiscal year; pre-tax cash flow of

Listing Requirement	*TSX Venture Tier 2 Issuers*	*TSX Venture Tier 1*	*TSX Non-exempt Exploration and Development Stage Issuers*	*TSX Non-exempt Producer Issuers*	*TSX Exempt Issuers*
				or documented historical production and financial performan	CAD700 000 in last fiscal year and average of CAD500 000 for past two fiscal years
Property	Qualifying Property (significant interest or in certain cases, a right to earn a signification interest). Sufficient evidence of no less than CAD100 000 of exploration expenditures on qualifying property in past three years	Tier 1 Property (material interest)	Advanced Exploration Property (minimum 50% interest)	Three years proven and probable reserves	Three years proven and probable reserves
Work Programme	CAD100 000 approved expenditures on the qualifying	CAD500 000 on the Tier 1 property	CAD750 000 on advanced exploration property	Bringing the mine into commercial production	Commercial level mining operations

Listing Requirement	*TSX Venture Tier 2 Issuers*	*TSX Venture Tier 1*	*TSX Non-exempt Exploration and Development Stage Issuers*	*TSX Non-exempt Producer Issuers*	*TSX Exempt Issuers*
	property within the thirty-six months preceding application of listing. CAD200 000 on the qualifying property				
Other Criteria	Geological report	Geological report	Management-prepared eighteen-month projection		Technical Report prepared by an independent qualified person
Distribution, Market Capitalization and Public Float	Public float of 500 000 shares; 200 public shareholders each holding a Board Lot* having no resale restrictions; 20% of issued and outstanding shares held by public shareholders	Public float of 1 000 000 shares; 250 public shareholders each holding a Board Lot* having no resale restrictions; 20% of issued and outstanding shares held by public shareholders	Market capitalization of CAD4 m; 1 000 000 free trading public shares; 300 public holders each holding a Board Lot*		

Industrial, Technology and Research & Development Companies: Overview of Selected Listing Requirements for Selected Issuers

Listing Requirement	*TSX Venture Tier 2 Industrial Technology Life Sciences Issuers*	*TSX Venture Tier 1 Industrial Technology Life Sciences Issuers*	*TSX Non-Exempt Technology Issuers*	*TSX Non-Exempt Research and Development (R&D) Issuers*	*TSX Exempt Issuers Industrial Companies*
Net Tangible Assets, Revenue	CAD750 000 in net tangible assets or CAD500 000 in revenue or CAD2 m arm's-length financing. Alternatively, if no revenue, a two-year management plan demonstrating reasonable likelihood of revenue within twenty-four months	CAD5 m in net tangible assets or CAD5 m revenue. Alternatively, if no revenue, a two-year management plan demonstrating reasonable likelihood of revenue within twenty-four months	No requirement	No requirement	CAD7.5 m of net tangible assets; Pretax earnings from ongoing operations of at least CAD300 000 in the last fiscal year
Working Capital and Capital Structure	Adequate working capital and financial resources to carry out	Adequate working capital and financial resources to carry out	Funds to cover all planned development expenditures,	Funds to cover all planned R&D expenditures, capital	Working capital to carry on the business, and an appropriate capital structure

Listing Requirement	*TSX Venture Tier 2 Industrial Technology Life Sciences Issuers*	*TSX Venture Tier 1 Industrial Technology Life Sciences Issuers*	*TSX Non-Exempt Technology Issuers*	*TSX Non-Exempt Research and Development (R&D) Issuers*	*TSX Exempt Issuers Industrial Companies*
	stated work programme or execute business plan for twelve months following listing; CAD100 000 unallocated funds	stated work programme or execute business plan for eighteen months following listing; CAD200 000 unallocated funds	capital expenditures, and general and administrative expenses for one year	expenditures, and general and administrative expenses for two years	
Cash Flow	No requirement	No requirement	No requirement	No requirement	Pre-tax cash flow of CAD700 000 in last fiscal year, and an average of CAD500 000 for past two fiscal years
Prior Expenditures and Work Programme	History of operations or validation of business				
Distribution, Market Capitalization and Public Float	Public float of 500 000 shares; 200 public shareholders each holding a	Public float of one million shares; 250 public shareholders each holding a	One million free trading public shares; CAD10 m held by	One million free trading public shares; CAD4 m held by	One million free trading public shares; CAD4 m held by

Listing Requirement	*TSX Venture Tier 2 Industrial Technology Life Sciences Issuers*	*TSX Venture Tier 1 Industrial Technology Life Sciences Issuers*	*TSX Non-Exempt Technology Issuers*	*TSX Non-Exempt Research and Development (R&D) Issuers*	*TSX Exempt Issuers Industrial Companies*
	'Board Lot'* having no resale restrictions; 20% of issued and outstanding shares held by public shareholders	'Board Lot'* having no resale restrictions; 20% of issued and outstanding shares held by public shareholders	public shareholders, 300 public shareholders each holding a 'Board Lot' Minimum CAD50 000 000 market capitalization	public shareholders, 300 public shareholders each holding a 'Board Lot'	public shareholders, 300 public shareholders each holding a 'Board Lot'

*A 'Board Lot' depends on the trading price of the shares. If the trading price per share is less than CAD0.10, the Board Lot size is 1 000 shares. If the trading price per unit is CAD0.10 to CAD0.99, the Board Lot size is 500 shares. If the trading price per unit is CAD1.00 or more, the Board Lot size is 100 shares.

In all cases noted above, the board of directors and management should have adequate experience and technical expertise relevant to the company's business and industry as well as adequate public company experience. In addition, the board of directors must have at least two independent directors.

There are several methods of listing on the TSX or TSXV. An issuer already listed on a stock exchange outside of Canada may apply for a dual listing. A private issuer may engage in a reverse merger (also known as a reverse takeover) with a Canadian public issuer. In a reverse merger, the Canadian public issuer will acquire the private issuer in a transaction in which the shares of the private issuer are exchanged for shares of the public issuer. An issuer may make an IPO through the distribution of securities under a prospectus in accordance with Canadian securities laws. Finally, a company seeking to list on the TSXV may engage in a 'qualifying transaction' with a capital pool company, which is essentially a listed company whose sole purpose is to conduct a reverse merger transaction.

2.3.4 Tipping and Insider Trading

[171] The Ontario *Securities Act* (along with the legislation of other provinces) prohibits tipping and insider trading. Persons or companies in a 'special relationship' with a reporting issuer are prohibited from purchasing or selling securities of the reporting issuer with the knowledge of a material fact or material change with respect to the reporting issuer that has not been generally disclosed. Persons and companies in a 'special relationship' with a reporting issuer are also prohibited from informing another person or company of a material fact or material change with respect to the reporting issuer before the material fact or material change has been generally disclosed, or recommending or encouraging another person or company to purchase or sell securities of the reporting issuer, unless the disclosure is in the necessary course of business.

Persons and companies who are in a special relationship with a reporting issuer encompass a wide variety of persons and entities. They include (among others):

- specified persons such as directors, officers, employees, of the reporting issuer, a subsidiary of the reporting issuer, or a person or company that controls, directly or indirectly, the reporting issuer;
- any person or company that is considering or evaluating whether to make a takeover bid or to become a party to a merger with the reporting issuer; and
- any person or company that learns of a material fact or material change with respect to the reporting issuer from any other person or company, and knows or ought reasonably to have known that the other person or company is in a 'special relationship' with the issuer.

[172] A 'material fact' is a fact that would reasonably be expected to have a significant effect on the market price or value of the securities. A 'material change' means a change in the business, operations or capital of the issuer that would reasonably be expected to have a significant effect on the market price or value of the securities. It also includes a decision to implement such a change by the board of directors or other persons acting in a similar capacity or by senior management who believe that confirmation of the decision by the board of directors is probable. The definition of 'material change' is slightly different where the issuer is an investment fund.

[173] Tipping and insider trading are offences punishable by a minimum fine equal to the profit made or the loss avoided by the person or company that committed the offence and a maximum fine equal to the greater of CAD5 m and triple the profit made or the loss avoided by the person or company that committed the offence.

[174] It is a criminal offence in Canada to knowingly convey inside information to another person knowing that there is a risk that the person will use the information to trade in securities. It is also a criminal offence to buy or sell a security using inside information. 'Inside information' is information relating to or affecting the issuer of a security or a security that the issuer has issued or is about to issue that: (a) has not been generally disclosed; and (b) would reasonably be expected to significantly affect the market price or value of the security. The punishment for tipping may be up to five years if convicted of an indictable offence and up to ten years imprisonment for insider trading.

2.4 Controls/Restrictions on Foreign Investment

2.4.1 Notification

[175] The *Investment Canada Act* requires notification and, in certain circumstances, review of investments by non-Canadians to establish new Canadian businesses or to acquire interests in existing Canadian businesses.

[176] A non-Canadian investor is a person (including a corporation or other legal entity), government, or government agency that is not Canadian. Whether a corporation is Canadian is frequently complex and depends on, among other things, whether the corporation is ultimately controlled or beneficially owned by individual Canadians. An individual is 'Canadian' if he or she is a Canadian citizen or permanent resident of Canada who has been ordinarily resident in Canada for not more than one year after the time at which he or she first became eligible to apply for Canadian citizenship.

[177] A non-Canadian establishing a new business or acquiring control of a business in Canada must file a notification with the Investment Review Division of Innovation, Science and Economic Development Canada, regardless of the size of the business. The notification must be filed prior to or within thirty days of the acquisition of control or of a new business becoming operative. In March 2024, significant amendments to the *Investment Canada Act* were enacted that will, among other things, expand the notification obligation to require a filing where a non-Canadian acquires any level of interest (including non-controlling interest) in an entity carrying on certain business activities to be defined by regulation, provided other specified conditions are met (such as the non-Canadian's ability to exercise certain rights and powers over the Canadian entity). Non-Canadians investing in such entities will also be required to file notifications on a pre-closing basis. As of July 2024, these amendments have not yet been brought into force by the Governor in Council order, nor have regulations listing the business activities attracting the expanded notification obligation been released. However, it is likely that investments in specific areas of the Canadian economy that have received more scrutiny from the federal government in recent years (e.g., supply chains for 'critical minerals' it deems important to Canada's economic and national security) will become subject to the new requirements.

[178] Certain types of acquisition of control are subject to review and approval by the minister responsible. The thresholds are:

(1) Direct Control of a Non-Cultural Canadian Business. The investment is made to directly acquire ownership and control of a non-cultural Canadian business and meets one of the following thresholds:
  - The investor is from certain countries with trade agreements with Canada (currently the US, EU members, the United Kingdom, Mexico, Brunei, Chile, Colombia, Panama, Peru, Honduras, South Korea, Japan, Malaysia, Vietnam, Singapore, Australia and New Zealand) and

the target company has an enterprise value of CAD1.989 bn (as of 2024; this amount is statutorily indexed to inflation).
- The investor is from a WTO member country and the target company has an enterprise value exceeding CAD1.287 bn (as of 2024; this amount is inflation-indexed).
- The investor is a state-owned enterprise (i.e., an entity owned or controlled, directly or indirectly, by a foreign government) (an 'SOE') and the asset value of the target exceeds CAD528 m (as of 2024; this amount is inflation-indexed). Upon the coming into force of the March 2024 amendments to the *Investment Canada Act* described above, the Governor in Council will also be able to require that a review takes place for SOE investments below this threshold if it considers such a review to be in the public interest.
- The investor is from a non-WTO country and the asset value of the target exceeds CAD5 m.

(2) Indirect Control of a Non-Cultural Canadian Business, where the Canadian business is acquired as a result of the acquisition of the non-Canadian parent company:
   - If the investor is from a non-WTO member country, the threshold is CAD50 m for indirect acquisitions.
   - Indirect acquisitions of most Canadian businesses by a WTO investor are not reviewable but are notifiable prior to closing or within thirty days of closing.

(3) Control of a Canadian Cultural Business:
   - The cultural business has an asset value of CAD5 m or more or the Government of Canada considers that the investment in a cultural business should be reviewed in the public interest.

(4) National Security:
   - The Government of Canada considers that the investment may be injurious to national security.

A 'cultural business' includes Canadian businesses carrying on one of the following activities:

- publication, distribution or sale of books, magazines, periodicals or newspapers in print or machine-readable form;
- production, distribution, sale or exhibition of film or video recordings or audio or video music recordings;
- publication, distribution or sale of music in print or machine-readable form;
- radio communication in which the transmissions are intended for direct reception by the general public, any radio, television and cable television broadcasting undertakings and any satellite programming and broadcast network services.

Applications for Review and the Review Process

[179] For reviewable investments, the investor must file an application for review to the applicable government agency and provide certain prescribed information.

If the acquisition of control is direct, the application must be filed before the transaction is completed and must include a description of the purchaser's plans for the Canadian business. The plans must also describe the 'net benefit' to Canada of the proposed investment. This should include any capital expenditure projections and the effect of the investment on employment, the location of the head office, technological development, competition and participation of Canadians in the senior management of the Canadian business.

[180] The Minister has an initial forty-five-day period to make a determination as to whether the investment is likely to be of 'net benefit' to Canada and whether to conduct a national security review. However, this period may be extended by the Minister unilaterally for a further thirty days. Any additional extensions must be with the consent of the investor. (Separate timing rules apply for national security reviews of investments, which are further described below.) A reviewable investment may not be completed prior to the investor receiving a decision from the Minister that the investment is of net benefit to Canada unless one of the following three exceptions applies:

(1) where the Minister is satisfied that a delay in implementing the investment would result in undue hardship to the investor or would jeopardize the operations of the Canadian business, and the Minister has sent a notice to the investor permitting implementation of the investment prior to completion of the review process;
(2) where the investment is an indirect acquisition; or
(3) where the investment is not normally reviewable, but the Government exercises its authority by Order-in-Council to review the investment because it involves a cultural business activity or, following the coming into force of the March 2024 amendments described above, because it is an SOE acquisition the review of which the Government determines to be in the public interest.

If the foreign investor completes the investment pursuant to one of the preceding exceptions and the Minister fails to approve it, the investor will be required to divest the investment.

Net Benefit to Canada Test

[181] If a transaction is reviewable, the Minister of Innovation, Science and Economic Development (or for cultural businesses, the Minister of Canadian Heritage) determines whether there is a 'net benefit' to Canada. The *Investment Canada Act* lists the following factors as relevant to determining whether there is a net benefit to Canada:

- the effect on the level of economic activity in Canada, on employment; on resource processing, on the utilization of parts and services produced in Canada and on exports from Canada;
- the degree and significance of participation by Canadians in Canadian business or new Canadian business and in any industry or industries in Canada;

- the effect of the investment on productivity, industrial efficiency, technological development, product innovation and product variety in Canada (with the March 2024 amendments to the *Investment Canada Act* set to clarify that this factor includes 'the effect of the investment on any rights relating to intellectual property whose development has been funded, in whole or in part, by the Government of Canada');
- the effect of the investment on competition within any industry in Canada;
- the compatibility of the investment with national industrial, economic and cultural policies (a factor that will likewise be amended to clarify that such policies are inclusive of 'industrial, economic and cultural policy objectives enunciated by the government or legislature of any province likely to be significantly affected by the investment, including the investment's effect on the use and protection of personal information about Canadians'); and
- the contribution of the investment to Canada's ability to compete in world markets.

[182] Where the Minister is not satisfied that the investment is not of net benefit to Canada, the investor will make additional representations and undertakings which would demonstrate the net benefit of investment. To the extent that the Minister remains unsatisfied, the investor will be notified of the Minister's position, and such investor will be prohibited from implementing the investment or will be required to divest itself of the investment if the investment has already been implemented. SOEs are subject to special considerations. The Minister will also review the corporate governance and commercial orientation of SOEs in determining whether reviewable acquisitions of control by SOEs are of net benefit to Canada. Factors that may be important are adherence to Canadian corporate governance standards and whether the business to be acquired by the SOE will continue to have the ability to operate on a commercial basis regarding matters such as export markets, capital expenditures, and research and development.

National Security Review

[183] Investments may also be reviewed on the basis of national security under a process applicable to both control and non-control investments. If the investment is considered to be injurious to national security, the Governor in Council may direct the purchaser not to implement the investment, direct a divestiture, or require undertakings as a condition of the investment. In order to trigger a national security review, within forty-five days of the date on which the notification or application for review has been filed and certified as complete, either (a) the Governor in Council must order a review of the transaction or (b) the Minister must issue a notice to the purchaser indicating that a review may be necessary on grounds of national security, in which case the Governor in Council has forty-five days from the date of notice to order a review. For transactions that require neither an application for review nor a notification, however, the Governor in Council or Minister can take these steps at any time within five years of the transaction's closing. To avoid the uncertainty of a potential post-closing national security review under such circumstances, investors may opt to file a voluntary notification, following which the relevant timeline is reduced to the same period applicable to mandatorily notified investments (forty-five days after the notification is certified as complete).In evaluating potential risks to national security under this framework,the Government has in recent years outlined a number of areas of specific concern in policy statements and guidance, including investments involving SOEs, ties to the Russian state, sensitive personal data, sensitive areas of technology (such as those with military or 'dual use' military-civilian applications), public health, 'critical minerals' it has designated as important to Canada's economic or national security and interactive digital media (such as video games and mobile apps), among others. As part of the above-referenced March 2024 amendments to the *Investment Canada Act* affecting certain investments by non-Canadians in entities carrying on business activities prescribed by regulation, such investments will not be allowed to close before the applicable timeline for a national security review expires.

2.4.2 Restricted Sectors

[184] There are a number of sectors of the Canadian economy with specific and occasionally highly technical rules for investment. The purpose of this section is to alert the reader to some of the basic issues in several of these sectors. This list of restricted sectors is non-exhaustive. A purchaser proposing to enter into one of these sectors is well-advised to seek early, detailed advice.

Financial Services

[185] The financial services sector is heavily regulated in Canada. Banking and the business of banking are within the exclusive jurisdiction of the federal Parliament. The Office of the Superintendent of Financial Institutions (commonly referred to as 'OSFI') is the primary regulator of banks and other federally incorporated financial institutions such as trust companies and credit unions. Provincial governments are also involved in the incorporation and regulation of certain types of provincial financial institutions, such as provincial trust companies and credit unions. Provincial governments (with exclusive jurisdiction over, *inter alia*, property and civil rights) also pass consumer protection legislation (which at least in one reported court decision has been held to apply to federally regulated banks).

[186] Canadian domestic banks, and Canadian bank subsidiaries of foreign banks wishing to carry on business in Canada, are incorporated pursuant to and governed by the federal *Bank Act*. Large domestic banks must be widely held and even medium-sized domestic banks must be at least 35% owned by the public. The *Bank Act* provides that no person is permitted to have a 'significant interest' (more than 10% of the issued shares of any class) except with the approval of the Minister of Finance, or as otherwise permitted in the *Bank Act*. Representatives from OSFI are active participants and supporters of the Financial Stability Board (FSB) including in the acceptance and implementation in Canada of the so-called Basel III capital adequacy regulations which the FSB has recommended as international standards. Canadian banks must adhere to minimum capital requirements and are subject to restrictions regarding their business and investment powers; as just one example Canadian banks are prohibited from sharing information about their clients with insurers to ensure separation of those industries. Foreign banks wishing to carry on business in Canada otherwise than through a Canadian bank subsidiary, have the alternative option of establishing a Canadian branch of the foreign bank with the required regulatory approvals from the Minister of Finance and OSFI. There is also the third option of establishing with regulatory approval a so-called representative office (which must remain passive). The permitted and restricted activities of both Canadian bank branches and representative offices of foreign banks are set out in the *Bank Act*.

Life Insurance Companies

[187] Insurance companies are heavily regulated by federal and provincial governments. There is significant foreign ownership in the property and casualty insurers. The OSFI has estimated that nearly half of the Canadian property and casualty insurance industry is foreign owned (by premium volume). By contrast, life insurance is dominated by three main conglomerates. Acquisition of certain demutualized insurance companies is restricted to 20% of the voting shares or up to 30% of the non-voting shares of these institutions, subject to certain conditions, including the prior receipt of ministerial approval.

Broadcasting

[188] Subject to various exemptions, broadcasting and broadcasting distribution are regulated in Canada by the Canadian Radio-television and Telecommunications Commission (CRTC) under the authority of the *Broadcasting Act* (Canada). A conventional television or radio programming undertaking licence provides the broadcaster with the right to transmit a signal on a defined frequency in a defined geographic area and at a defined power level. Distribution undertaking licences (cable, direct-to-home or Internet Protocol television) licences permit the retransmission of programming in defined geographic areas. Pay television, pay-per-view, video-on-demand and specialty services are subject to prior Commission approval before they may be distributed by a licensed distribution undertaking. Broadcasting licences are not to be issued to non-Canadians or to companies that are effectively controlled by non-Canadians. The *Broadcasting Act* imposes an aggregate limit on foreign ownership of a broadcasting licensee to 20% of the issued voting shares. In 2023, the *Broadcasting Act* was amended to grant the CRTC specific authority to impose regulatory obligations on 'online undertakings' transmitting programming over internet-based video or audio streaming services. These changes do not require such online undertakings to obtain a broadcasting licence to which the ownership restrictions noted above would apply. However, as part of its ongoing implementation of the new framework, the CRTC issued a June 2024 decision requiring online undertakings that earn Canadian revenues of CAD25 m or more (subject to certain revenue exclusions set out in its decision) and that are not affiliated with a Canadian broadcaster to contribute 5% of those revenues to various funds supporting Canadian and Indigenous content. The CRTC noted that this requirement would 'level the playing field' between foreign owners of streaming services and traditional Canadian broadcasters competing in the space, which have long been subject to similar contribution requirements with respect to their legacy television, distribution and radio businesses.

Telecommunications

[189] As with broadcasting, telecommunications services are regulated by the CRTC. The CRTC administers the *Telecommunications Act*. Traditionally, facilities-based telecommunications companies in Canada had similar foreign ownership restrictions to those in the broadcasting sector. However, 2012 amendments directed at more fully opening Canada's telecommunications markets to foreign investment have since exempted a telecommunications common carrier if the carrier and all its affiliates have total annual telecommunications revenues representing less than 10% of total Canadian telecommunications revenues, as determined by the CRTC. Foreign ownership in carriers that do not qualify for this exemption is limited, in aggregate, to 20% of the issued voting shares.

Air Transportation

[190] The *Canada Transportation Act* contains airline ownership restrictions requiring air carriers operating or proposing to operate a domestic air service to be Canadian unless they obtain an exemption from the Minister of Transportation. Non-Canadians are eligible to hold licences for scheduled international air service if the non-Canadian is operating under the terms agreed to in an agreement between a foreign government and the federal government of Canada. A corporation is Canadian if it is incorporated or formed under the laws of Canada or a province, 51% of its voting interests are owned and controlled by Canadians (with no individual foreign investor holding more than 25% and foreign air carriers, collectively, holding no more than 25%) and it is controlled in fact by Canadians.

Real Estate

[191] In some cases, foreign ownership of land may be restricted in Canada. For example, limits have been established on the ownership of certain agricultural and recreational land in Alberta by an individual who is not a Canadian citizen or a permanent resident, the government of a country other than Canada or a political subdivision of a country other than Canada, or any agency of such government or political subdivision, or a corporation incorporated elsewhere than in Canada.

2.4.3 Foreign Extraterritorial Measures Act

[192] The *Foreign Extraterritorial Measures Act* (FEMA) is a blocking statute designed to prevent the application of foreign laws to Canadian trade interests. FEMA authorizes the Attorney General to make orders relating to measures of foreign states or foreign tribunals affecting international trade or commerce.

[193] To date, only two orders have been made under this Act. The first is an order relating to the attempt of the US to restrict trade and commerce between Canada and Cuba. The Cuba Order provides that every Canadian corporation and every director and officer of a Canadian corporation must give notice to the Attorney General of Canada of any directive, instruction, intimation of policy or other communication relating to an extraterritorial measure of the US in respect of any trade or commerce between Canada and Cuba that the Canadian corporation, director or officer has received from a person who is in a position to direct or influence the policies of the Canadian corporation in Canada. This order also prohibits any Canadian corporation from complying with any extraterritorial measure of the US relating to Canada's trade with Cuba.

[194] The second order, commonly known as the 'Buy American Order', prohibits any person in Canada from complying with the US 'Buy America' requirements in relation to the redevelopment of the Prince Rupert ferry terminal facility in British Columbia. The order responds to a solicitation for bids issued by the Alaska Department of Transportation and Public Facilities which specified that all iron and steel products associated with the ferry redevelopment project would be subject to the US 'Buy America' legislation.

2.4.4 Expropriation

[195] Canadian federal and provincial laws permit expropriation for a public purpose. However, governments are obligated to pay compensation unless legislation specifically provides otherwise. Generally, expropriation is not a significant issue in Canada except with respect to real property, which may be required for planning and redevelopment purposes. A high-profile exception involved the insolvency of Abitibi-Bowater. Prior to seeking creditor protection, the Legislature of Newfoundland and Labrador passed legislation that transferred most of the company's property in the province to the province without any legal remedy. This occurred on the eve of the company seeking protection under the CCAA. The company then brought a NAFTA claim, as they were US nationals, which the federal government subsequently settled for CAD130 m.

2.4.5 Financing

[196] Most Canadian financing is obtained from banks and institutional lenders, which are generally willing to finance large-scale investments. In addition, debt financing may be obtained by offering debt securities (promissory notes or debentures) in the Canadian capital markets. Operating loans are frequently revolving and payable on a demand basis, although some operating loans may have a term. Term loans are usually paid in instalments over time, subject to a lender's right to accelerate the entire loan balance upon the occurrence of one or more specified events of default. For more information on financing options, *see* 'Debt Financing'. It should be noted that Canadian companies are permitted to hold offshore bank accounts.

[197] Generally, there are no restrictions on non-bank foreign lenders extending loans to Canadians and obtaining the necessary security over both movable and immovable property. There are also no exchange or currency controls that restrict payments to a foreign lender under a security agreement. However, the *Bank Act* prohibits a foreign bank from carrying on banking business in Canada without satisfying the applicable legislative or regulatory requirements and approvals. Furthermore, Canada imposes reporting requirements for anti-money laundering and terrorist financing controls which apply to a broad range of businesses, including banks and money services businesses. In addition, most provinces require mortgage brokers and dealers to be licensed.

2.5 Incentives for Foreign Investment

[198] Canadian governments generally do not specifically target investment incentives for foreign capital but instead aim to attract capital based on Canada's stable government, economy and financial institutions. However, governments do offer numerous incentives to attract investment into specific areas or sectors. For example, Québec's 'Plan d'action nordique' (Northern Action Plan) is a multi-year investment initiative to develop infrastructure, promote natural resources and other economic development projects, invest in local communities and ensure the protection of ecosystems in Northern Québec.

[199] Although there are generally no restrictions on the repatriation of profits, there are withholding taxes of 25% on the payment of dividends unless the rate is reduced under a tax treaty. Canada's tax treaties may reduce the rate of withholding taxes substantially, particularly for a foreign resident corporate shareholder. The repatriation of profits through shareholder loans is subject to certain deeming rules that result in loans to a foreign shareholder being treated as a dividend and subject to a withholding tax unless certain exceptions relating to the length of the loan apply.

2.5.1 Free Trade Agreements and Bilateral Investment Treaties

[200] Canada is party to a number of free trade agreements as well as Bilateral Investment Treaties which are referred to in Canada as Foreign Investment Protection and Promotion Agreements (FIPPAs). These agreements liberalize trade and promote and protect foreign investment in Canada and the reciprocating country.

[201] Canada began negotiating FIPPAs based on a model agreement developed by the Organization for Economic Cooperation and Development (OECD). Canadian FIPPAs typically protect against discrimination, guarantee the minimum standard of treatment under international law, and compensation upon expropriation, among other investment protections. Investors have the ability to directly bring a claim before a panel of arbitrators under the framework provided by either the International Centre for the Settlement of Investment Disputes, the United Nations Commission on International Trade Law (UNCITRAL) Arbitration Rules or other agreed-upon arbitration rules against a treaty party for a breach of an obligation owed to the investor. The federal government is liable for any breaches of obligations committed by all levels of government included within the scope of a treaty.

NAFTA and the Canada- United States- Mexico Agreement

[202] Prior to 1 July 2020, the North American Free Trade Agreement (NAFTA), which was in effect since 1 January 1994 and was signed by Canada, the US, and

Mexico, was arguably Canada's most important international trade agreement. However, NAFTA was negotiated and a new agreement, the Canada- United States-Mexico Agreement (CUSMA), was concluded and signed on 30 November 2018. The CUSMA entered into force on 1 July 2020 and replaced the NAFTA. The CUSMA includes updated rules of origin, specifically for the automotive sector, increased dairy market access into Canada, increased protections for intellectual property, increased *de minimis* thresholds for sales tax and customs duties on imports for Canada and Mexico, and a new chapter on digital trade. One notable difference is the lack of investment dispute resolution provisions between Canada and the US. Under the CUSMA Canadian and US investors will not be able to bring claims against each other's host state. Further, Canada is not a party to the CUSMA's chapter on procurement, leaving the WTO Agreement on Government Procurement to govern procurement between Canada and the US once the NAFTA is no longer applicable.

The CUSMA keeps in place the main features of NAFTA in relation to goods:

- National Treatment. The parties agree to accord national treatment to the goods and services of other parties. This includes prohibiting the imposition or application of measures to afford protection to domestic production or domestic industries. There are exceptions. In Canada, these exceptions include treatment with respect to the exportation of logs of all species as well as some unprocessed fish based on provincial laws, excise duties on the absolute volume of ethyl alcohol, prohibited goods, the use of ships in the coasting trade of Canada, and quantitative restrictions to certain US originating goods.
- Tariff Elimination. Tariffs on virtually all originating goods traded between Canada, the US and Mexico, remain at zero.

World Trade Organization

[203] Canada is also a member of the WTO, the international body dealing with the global rules of trade between nations. Canada is bound by the WTO Agreements which form the basis of the multilateral trading system. These agreements embody the legal ground rules governing international commerce. As with other trade and investment agreements entered into by Canada, the federal government may be liable for breaches of obligations committed by a province.

Canada: EU Comprehensive Economic and Trade Agreement and Canada-United Kingdom Trade Continuity Agreement

[204] The Canada and EU Comprehensive Economic and Trade Agreement (CETA) is an agreement with the EU. CETA covers all aspects of Canada's broad trading relationship with the EU, including goods, services, investment, government procurement and regulatory cooperation. CETA provisionally entered into force in September 2017, and save for certain investment, financial services and intellectual property provisions, the entire agreement has been operational since that time. Following the exit of the United Kingdom (UK) from the EU on 31 January 2020, Canada entered into the Canada-United Kingdom Trade Continuity Agreement with the UK on 1 April 2021, to preserve the benefits of CETA between the UK and Canada and maintain preferential access to the UK market. While Canada and the UK have attempted to negotiate a free trade agreement to replace the continuity agreement, these negotiations reached an impasse in early 2024, with UK negotiators walking away from the talks.

Comprehensive and Progressive Agreement for Trans-Pacific Partnership

[205] The *Comprehensive and Progressive Agreement for Trans-Pacific Partnership* (CPTPP) is a trade agreement among eleven Pacific Rim countries including Australia, Brunei Darussalam, Canada, Chile, Japan, Malaysia, Mexico, New Zealand, Peru, Singapore and Vietnam. The CPTPP is the largest trade agreement negotiated in the last twenty years and is expected to substantially reduce barriers to trade and investment among its member countries. The expansive thirty-chapter trade agreement covers digital trade and e-commerce, investment, procurement, supply chain goods and rules of origin, and services including financial services, among others.

[206] The CPTPP entered into force on 30 December 2018 for Australia, Canada, Japan, Mexico, New Zealand, and Singapore. The Agreement entered into force on 14 January 2019 for Vietnam, on 19 September 2021 for Peru, 29 November 2022 for Malaysia, on 21 February 2023 for Chile and on 13 May 2023 for Brunei.

[207] Notably, the CPTPP may continue to expand its reach over the coming years with various countries indicating interest in joining. The UK formally signed the CPTPP's accession protocol in mid-2023 and the CPTPP is slated to come into force in the country once all original CPTPP parties ratify its accession. Several other countries, including China, Taiwan, Ecuador, Costa Rica, Uruguay and Ukraine, have also made formal applications to accede to the agreement.

2.6 Specific Issues of Company Law

2.6.1 Incorporators

[208] Any person or corporation may seek to incorporate a corporation pursuant to the CBCA. There is no residency requirement for the incorporator but the directors of the company must satisfy the residency requirements. If the incorporator is an individual, he or she must be at least 18 years of age, not of unsound mind, and not a bankrupt.

[209] It is possible for an incorporator or other promoter of a corporation to enter into a contract on behalf of the corporation prior to it becoming incorporated. Given the speed with which companies may be incorporated, this is less frequent today than in the past. However, it may arise in mergers and acquisitions when a company may wish to enter into an agreement to acquire another company through the incorporation of a wholly owned subsidiary but does not yet wish to commit to the trouble or expense of incorporation in the event that the transaction is not approved.

[210] Unless the incorporator or other promoter expressly disclaims personal liability upon entering into a pre-incorporation contract, personal liability will be assumed. Upon incorporation, the corporation may signify by action or conduct an intention to be bound by the contract.

2.6.2 Corporate Name

[211] Every corporation must have a legal name by which it does business and under which it may sue and be sued. Incorporators may choose a name or be assigned a numbered company name upon incorporation. There is considerable flexibility in the choice of name provided that it is unique, does not consist entirely of symbols, and is in English or French. A corporation may also use a name other than its assigned name provided that this name is registered to the corporation. It is possible, therefore, for a corporation to do business simultaneously under several names. A corporation may also change its legal name by way of an amendment to its articles. The change of name does not affect the continuity of the corporation.

2.6.3 Constating Documents

Certificate of Incorporation

[212] A company becomes incorporated pursuant to the CBCA upon the issuance of a certificate of incorporation. The certificate is issued by the Director appointed under the CBCA (which should not be confused with the directors of the corporation). The issuance of the certificate creates a juristic person separate from that of its incorporators and shareholders. The corporation is deemed to have all of the rights, powers and privileges of a natural person.

Articles

[213] The articles of incorporation of CBCA companies are the basic charter documents of the corporation. The articles provide basic information and characteristics of the corporation including:

- name;
- location of registered office;
- classes of shares and any restrictions on transfers of shares;
- number of directors (and first directors); and
- less commonly, restrictions on the business that the corporation may carry on.

The filing is an over-the-counter or online procedure and registration can usually be completed on the same date that the articles of incorporation are filed.

By-Laws

[214] The by-laws of a CBCA corporation provide the governance framework for the corporation, subject to the requirements of the incorporating statute. Subject to the provisions of the articles and statutory requirements, the by-laws describe the composition of the board of directors, the offices of the corporation, the manner of

calling board and shareholder meetings, quorum requirements for meetings, and the terms of any special rights and restrictions attaching to various classes of shares. Subject to confirmation at the next shareholders' meeting, the directors may make, amend or repeal by-laws, unless the articles, a unanimous shareholder agreement (described next) or the by-laws specify otherwise.

Unanimous Shareholder Agreements

[215] Shareholders of a CBCA corporation may restrict the powers of the directors (in whole or in part) to manage the business and affairs of the corporation, through a unanimous shareholders agreement. Such an agreement is useful with respect to subsidiary corporations so that it may be managed on a day-to-day basis by the parent company. It is also useful in other closely held corporations, where the shareholders are active owners. If the shareholders relieve the directors of their duties and responsibilities, the shareholders become liable in place of the directors in respect of those duties and responsibilities.

Corporate Seal

[216] Typically a corporation will have a corporate seal. However, a corporation need not use a corporate seal to enter into a contract or make a deed. In the event the parties to a contract require a seal, the contract may be sealed in the same manner as a contract would be signed under seal by an individual.

2.6.4 Shares

[217] Business corporations are organized as share capital corporations. A share is the ownership interest of a shareholder. A share is a fractional part of the capital of a corporation which confers upon the holder a certain right to a proportionate part of the capital of the corporation, whether by way of dividend or upon a distribution on the dissolution of the corporation and governs the right to vote at shareholder meetings. Shareholders do not have an interest in the underlying assets of the corporation. It represents the fractional part of the income and capital of a corporation that the shareholder is entitled to by way of dividend or upon liquidation or dissolution, in each case subject to the express rights or limitations on those rights in the articles of the corporation.

[218] The share capitalization of a corporation may be very flexible and can be tailored to meet its specific requirements. A corporation may have more than one class of shares and may have classes of shares with conversion rights into other classes of shares. If there is only one class of shares, all such shares must carry an equal right to vote at meetings of shareholders, receive dividends and participate in the distribution of the assets upon the dissolution of the corporation. However, it is also possible to create more than one class of shares with different rights or ranking behind another class, provided that at least one class of shares has the right to vote at meetings of shareholders and at least one class has the right to receive the remaining property of the corporation upon dissolution.

[219] The articles of a corporation may restrict or provide for an unlimited number of shares of a particular class. Shares do not have a par value and are non-assessable (although a shareholder may enter into a contract or shareholders agreement in which the shareholder agrees to subscribe for additional shares or invest additional equity). Shares must be fully paid up in money or money's worth in the form of property or past services when issued. Property does not include a promissory note or a promise to pay if it is issued by the subscriber of the share or a person who does not deal at arm's length to the person who is issued the share. This may be important in certain acquisition structures because it means that a parent company may not take back shares in a subsidiary on the issuance of a promissory note to the subsidiary.

[220] Shares may have (and typically all private company shares do have) restrictions on their transfer. In the absence of such a restriction, shares are presumed to be freely transferable.

[221] Dividends are payable, at the discretion of the directors, out of the distributable profits of the company. Dividends can only be declared after the corporation has satisfied the solvency test which requires the corporation to be able to pay its liabilities before they become due and to ensure that the net realizable value of its assets does not exceed its liabilities. Corporations are also able to redeem their shares upon satisfying the solvency test.

2.6.5 Requirement to Track Beneficial Ownership, Control or Direction

[222] In 2019, the CBCA was amended to: (i) increase transparency as to the individuals who own or control corporations; (ii) assist investigators in exposing money laundering, tax evasion and terrorist financing; and (iii) help Canada meet its international obligations. As a result of these changes, CBCA corporations are now required to create and maintain a register or list of individuals who exercise 'significant control' over the corporation, whether directly or indirectly (an 'ISC Register'). An indirect relationship of this nature is often referred to as 'beneficial' ownership or control.

[223] Under the current law, a CBCA corporation is required to maintain in its corporate records a list of registered owners of its shares, being the persons named on its share certificates. Through the implementation of the ISC Register, CBCA corporations are also required to keep a record of any individual(s) who exercises significant control over the corporation, i.e., an ISC Register. This is aimed at capturing information about beneficial owners, being individual(s) with ultimate ownership or control of the corporation, who are sometimes not the registered owners.

[224] An 'individual with significant control', or 'ISC', includes any individual, or any group of individuals acting 'jointly or in concert', who owns or controls 25% or more of the voting rights attached to a corporation's shares or 25% or more of the corporation's shares by value. The rule also provides that any individual who has influence that, if exercised, would result in 'control in fact' over the corporation is an ISC.

[225] A CBCA corporation is required to identify ISCs and then gather the following in respect of each such individual for inclusion in the ISC Register:

- name, date of birth and latest known address;
- jurisdiction for tax purposes;
- the day on which she or he acquired or ceased to have significant control over the corporation; and
- a description of how such control is maintained.

[226] The corporation will also be required, at least annually, to take 'reasonable steps' to identify ISCs and to ensure the information in the ISC Register is accurate, complete and up-to-date. Those steps must be recorded in the ISC Register. If the corporation becomes aware of information required to be included in the ISC Register, it is obligated to update the ISC Register within fifteen days of having become aware of it.

[227] The only CBCA corporations that are exempt from these requirements are reporting issuers or those listed on a designated stock exchange. The policy rationale is that significant shareholders of such corporations are obliged to make public disclosure of their shareholdings. Wholly owned subsidiaries of corporations listed on a designated stock exchange are not exempted.

[228] A shareholder or creditor of a non-exempted CBCA corporation will be entitled to access the corporation's ISC Register, but only in connection with a matter 'relating to the affairs' of the corporation, which includes: (a) an effort to influence a shareholder vote, or (b) an offer to acquire securities of the corporation. The Director of the CBCA will be entitled to access the ISC Register, though, in reality, this is unlikely as Corporations Canada is not an investigative body.

[229] The Canada Revenue Agency and the police are also permitted to access the ISC Register in certain circumstances, primarily, in the event the authorities have reasonable grounds to suspect both that: (a) the corporation or an ISC is implicated in an offence, and (b) the ISC Register or parts of it would be relevant to investigating that offence.

[230] Any knowing authorization, permission or acquiescence in contravention of the duties set out in the legislation by a director, officer or shareholder of the corporation constitutes an offence and could result in a fine of up to CAD200 000, up to six months of jail time, or both.

[231] Since 2019, all provinces in Canada except Alberta have introduced corporate transparency registers. The three territories, Yukon, Northwest Territories and Nunavut are yet to require corporate transparency registers.

2.6.6 Share Certificates

[232] A share certificate is proof of the title of the shareholder to the shares issued to the shareholder. The by-laws of the corporation may provide that shares will be book entry only. This is increasingly typical of public companies.

2.6.7 Warrants and Options

[233] A corporation may grant warrants or options to acquire shares. The holder of options or warrants is not a shareholder of the corporation and has no rights to vote on or participate in the corporation until the warrant or option is exercised.

2.6.8 Debt Financing

[234] In simple terms, debt is an obligation to pay a liquidated sum of money. Unless the articles, by-laws or a unanimous shareholder agreement restrict the authority of the corporation to borrow, the directors of a corporation may, without authorization of the shareholders, cause the corporation to borrow money or guarantee an obligation and may cause the corporation to grant security over the corporation's assets. The board of directors may delegate this authority to one or more directors or officers. In addition, corporations will typically have specific borrowing provisions in their by-laws or a special 'banking' by-law.

[235] To raise capital, a corporation may also issue debt securities, including notes, debentures and bonds. These securities may be issued pursuant to trust indentures and may include conversion rights into shares of the corporation or warrant provisions. In some cases, the debt securities may be repayable in shares of the corporation upon the occurrence of specific events or at the option of either the creditor or the corporation.

[236] Some obligations of a corporation may have features of both debt and equity. Distinguishing between these types of obligations will be important in liquidation or insolvency proceedings as well as in situations in which solvency requirements must be met for certain corporate actions. For example, a corporation may not redeem shares or pay dividends without meeting solvency requirements. There are no similar requirements in respect of debt obligations. This may be an important consideration for distributions from a subsidiary to a parent company.

[237] In most cases, lenders will often request security for their loans. In some cases, lenders will require guarantees from the shareholders, subsidiaries or other related parties. Common types of security which banks and other institutional lenders in Canada may require are:

- a general security agreement creating a security interest in all of the borrower's (or guarantor's) present and after-acquired property, assets and undertaking;
- a mortgage/charge of real property;
- a debenture charging all present and after-acquired property, assets and undertaking of the borrower (or guarantor), which can include a specific mortgage and charge of real property;
- a pledge of securities whereby the equity of the borrower, guarantor or their respective subsidiaries is taken as collateral;
- security under section 426 or 427 of the *Bank Act* (Canada), which provides for the creation and granting of special inventory security; and
- a general assignment of accounts receivable.

As in many jurisdictions, the concept of a 'floating charge' over all assets of a debtor company exists in the form of a general security agreement that creates interests in all of the debtor's present and after-acquired property.

Real Property and Personal Property

[238] Security may be taken over real and personal property in Canada. In all parts of Canada other than Québec, security is taken over real property through a mortgage or charge registered on title in either a land titles or registry system. In Québec, security is taken through a hypothec. Once registered, the lender generally has priority over subsequent encumbrances.

[239] Canada has largely harmonized its system for taking security over personal property, which includes equipment, inventory, accounts receivable, shares and intangibles. In all provinces and territories other than Quebec, this legislation is called *the Personal Property Security Act* (PPSA). As Quebec is a civil law jurisdiction, the Province of Quebec's system is slightly different but does provide for a registry of security interests in personal property. The comments in this section are based on the Ontario PPSA.

[240] In addition to general security over personal property, the PPSA applies to a lease that secures payment or performance of an obligation and any lease of goods with a term that is greater than one year. It also applies to a transfer of an account or chattel paper, whether or not the transfer secures payment or performance of an obligation.

Attachment and Perfection under the PPSA

[241] The PPSA establishes the requirements for 'attachment' of a security interest to the collateral. There are specific provisions in the PPSA establishing the requirements for attachment. Once the security interest has attached, it is necessary to 'perfect' the security interest in order to obtain priority over other security interests. Perfection can be accomplished through possession of the collateral, through obtaining control over securities or, more commonly, through registration of a financing statement.

[242] In addition to the PPSA, most Canadian provinces and territories have adopted securities transfer legislation, such as the Ontario *Securities Transfer Act, 2006*, to govern the transfer and holding of financial assets, which include (among other things) securities and interests in securities. This legislation accommodates the reality that securities of public companies are typically not held by the beneficial owner in a certificated form. Instead, the shares are held in book form – that is, recorded in books of a securities intermediary. The *Securities Transfer Act* permits a holder to perfect security over investment property, such as uncertificated securities, securities accounts, and securities entitlements, by way of 'control'. Perfection by control may be accomplished in a number of ways depending on the type of financial asset, including by entering into a control agreement. Although these methods are available, in many transactions, a lender will require that securities that are not publicly traded be certificated and control established in the traditional manner of possession.

[243] Each province maintains its own real and personal property registries. In preparation for an acquisition of a business, it may be necessary to conduct registry searches in each province or territory in which the borrower has assets or where the debtor may otherwise be deemed to be located to determine whether the assets being purchased are subject to a security interest.

Bank Act Security

[244] Canadian banks have the right to take a specific type of security under the *Bank Act* (Canada). This security can be taken and perfected throughout the country. It permits the bank to take charge of the debtor's inventory, receivables generated from the sale of products and other limited classes of property. Canadian banks may take this special *Bank Act* security from debtors who are manufacturers or who are wholesale and retail purchasers or shippers of, and dealers in, farm, mine, and sea products. *Bank Act* security is also available with respect to loans and advances made on the security of hydrocarbons and minerals, which may be useful in the oil, gas and mining sectors.

Priorities

[245] Priorities among secured creditors are usually determined by order of perfection. There are some exceptions. For example, a 'purchase-money security interest' or 'PMSI' is a type of security interest taken to secure payment of part of the purchase price of the collateral. A PMSI creditor may achieve super priority over other types of security interests in that collateral even if the PMSI creditor did not register first. In the insolvency context, certain preferential creditors will rank ahead of all secured creditors. These preferences may include claims for professional fees, unpaid employee wages, administrative fees, rent payments under a commercial lease and certain taxes.

Rights on Default

[246] The PPSA contains comprehensive rules dealing with the respective rights and obligations of a creditor and debtor following default by a debtor. These rights include the right to take possession of, to retain and to dispose of the collateral, all of which are readily enforceable. Debtors have the right to redeem the collateral and to receive notice of the creditor's intentions with respect to the collateral, among other rights. Canadian courts are unlikely to set aside or disregard a security interest; however, secured creditors may lose priority in the insolvency context if preferential creditors exist. For more information on enforcement, *see* the '*Receivership*' section below.

2.6.9 Duties of the Directors and Officers

[247] Directors and officers must act honestly and in good faith with a view to the best interests of the corporation. This is referred to as the duty of loyalty. The duty of loyalty is owed to the corporation and not to the shareholders or any particular constituency of the corporation. This means that a director must act in the best interests of the corporation even if that is in conflict with the interests of his or her nominating shareholder. This does not mean, however, that directors and officers do not have to consider the impact of a decision on a corporation's stakeholders. Depending on the circumstances, directors and officers may be required to demonstrate that stakeholder interests were taken into account.

[248] The duty of loyalty includes a duty to maintain the confidence of the corporation, a duty to maximize the long-run value of the corporation's business and a duty to avoid conflicts of interest, including a duty not to take corporate opportunities for the director's own benefit.

[249] Directors and officers must also exercise the care, diligence and skill that a reasonably prudent person would exercise in comparable circumstances. This is referred to as the duty of care. Directors are permitted to rely on officers and outside advisors. However, the reliance must be reasonable. Typically, directors and officers must put into place compliance programmes to support a due diligence defence to a plethora of liabilities, discussed in the next section.

[250] Each of these duties continues to apply to directors engaged in an M&A transaction. However, additional disclosure requirements may apply including the obligation to distribute management information circulars. For more information on directors' duties in the context of M&A and hostile transactions *see* the '*Directors' Circular*' section below.

2.6.10 Liabilities of Directors and Officers

[251] Directors and officers are subject to numerous potential liabilities. In Ontario alone, a director or officer might theoretically be subject to more than a hundred statutes imposing specific duties and liabilities. The range of potential liabilities depends on the industry in which the corporation operates and the extent of its operations. In some cases, directors may invoke a 'due diligence' defence. A 'due diligence' defence requires that the director or officer demonstrate that he or she took reasonable steps to avoid the breach or event for which the director or officer would otherwise be liable. The level of diligence is a question of mixed fact and law for the court.

[252] The following are the most common types of potential liability to apply to most directors and officers of CBCA corporations.

Wages-Related Liabilities

[253] Under the CBCA, directors are jointly and severally liable to employees of the corporation for all debts not exceeding six months' wages payable to each employee for services performed for the corporation while they are such directors respectively. Under Ontario's *Employment Standards Act, 2000* (ESA), directors are also liable for unpaid overtime, holiday pay as well as vacation pay accrued for up to twelve months during the time in which they were directors. However, under the ESA, directors are not liable for termination pay or severance pay. Typically, outside of situations of bankruptcy or liquidation, the director is not liable unless: (a) the employee sues the corporation within six months of the wages becoming due and execution has been returned unsatisfied in whole or in part; and (b) the employee sues the director within two years after the director ceases to be a director.

Pension Liabilities

[254] Employee pension plans are subject to legislation that may impose liabilities on directors and officers. For example, Ontario's *Pension Benefits Act* requires corporate employers to hold employee contributions in trust. Directors and officers who cause, authorize, permit, acquiesce or participate in a breach may incur fines of up to CAD100 000 on a first conviction and up to CAD200 000 subsequently. Directors who fail to take reasonable care to prevent a corporation from committing an offence may also face potential liability for shortfalls as a result of a breach of their fiduciary obligations.

Source Deductions and Employer Premiums

[255] Income tax legislation and a variety of federal or provincial social programme legislation may require a corporation to deduct and remit taxes or to pay premiums with respect to the corporation's payroll. These include income tax payments, Canada Pension Plan payments, Employment Insurance premiums and provincial health taxes. Directors may be jointly and severally liable to pay these amounts if the corporation fails to comply with these obligations.

[256] Before the Canada Revenue Agency is entitled to pursue a director for federal unpaid source deductions, the Canada Revenue Agency must satisfy one of the following preconditions: (a) the Canada Revenue Agency has received a certificate from the Federal Court of Canada showing the amount of the unpaid source deductions after attempted execution against the company for six months; (b) the company has commenced liquidation or dissolution proceedings or has been dissolved and a claim for unpaid source deductions was proven within six months of the commencement of the proceedings or the dissolution (whichever is earlier); or (c) the corporation has made an assignment in bankruptcy or had a bankruptcy order made against it and a claim for the unpaid source deductions was proven within six months of the data of the assignment or order. A former director is not liable for federal unpaid source deductions more than two years after ceasing to be a director.

Occupational Health and Safety

[257] Occupational health and safety in Canada are regulated by both the federal and provincial governments. Federal health and safety legislation applies to federally regulated employers and imposes liability on directors and officers for failure to comply with the legislation. Provincial occupational health and safety legislation imposes liability on directors and officers of provincially regulated employers. For example, the Ontario *Occupational Health and Safety Act* (OHSA) imposes liability on directors and officers for failure to act reasonably to ensure the corporation acts in compliance with the OHSA and regulations. In Ontario, directors and officers may be subject to a fine of up to CAD1.5 m, twelve months' imprisonment, or both. It is important for directors and officers to ensure a reporting system is in place that maintains compliance with the OHSA and adequately addresses issues that may arise.

[258] In addition, directors and officers may be liable under section 217.1 of the *Criminal Code* if they do not take reasonable steps to prevent bodily harm to an employee arising from work or a task that the employee is directed to perform. In addition, directors and officers who are the 'directing minds' of a corporation may be liable for criminal negligence.

Goods and Services Tax and Harmonized Sales Tax

[259] The *Excise Tax Act* imposes value added taxes on supplies of goods and services in Canada. In provinces that have harmonized their provincial sales tax with the federal value added tax, the combined tax is referred to as Harmonized Sales Tax (HST). In other provinces, the federal tax is referred to as goods and services tax (GST). The *Excise Tax Act* requires that companies remit net tax owing to the Receiver General of Canada. If the corporation fails to do so, directors who were in office at the time are jointly and severally liable to pay the net tax. A former director is not liable for unremitted GST/HST more than two years after ceasing to be a director. However, this period may continue indefinitely if the director is a de facto director – that is, an individual who exercises apparent authority as a director even though that person was not formally elected or appointed in accordance with the constating documents for the corporation or, if properly elected or appointed, did not cease to exercise those powers following resignation. Therefore, it is important to properly resign and terminate the participation in the governance of the company to avoid the potential for continuing liability.

Environmental Liabilities

[260] Directors and officers may be held principally liable or as the controlling minds of the corporation for the environmental consequences of a corporation's activities. For example, under the *Canadian Environmental Protection Act* (CEPA), a corporation's officers, directors and agents, as well as the corporation itself, may be liable if they knew or ought to have known that their corporation was in contravention of CEPA but failed to take steps to prevent the contravention from occurring. There are numerous provincial statutes imposing environmental liabilities. In Ontario, these include the *Environmental Protection Act,* the *Ontario Water Resources Act* and the *Pesticides Act.* Provincial standards for directors and officers may go beyond federal legislation. In Ontario, for example, directors must take all reasonable care to prevent environmental offences. The maximum fines for offences under provincial environmental statutes can be significant. For example, under the Ontario *Environmental Protection Act,* directors and officers convicted of certain offences can be liable for up to CAD4 m on a first conviction and up to CAD6 m subsequently.

Dividends & Share Redemptions

[261] Directors may be liable under the CBCA for dividends paid or share redemptions made when the corporation was unable to satisfy the corporate solvency tests. Similarly, directors may be liable under the *Bankruptcy and Insolvency Act*

(BIA) for dividends or for redeemed shares where payment was made one year preceding bankruptcy and the corporation was insolvent at the time the payment was made or rendered insolvent as a result of making the payment.

Insider Trading

[262] Under the CBCA, provincial securities legislation, and the *Criminal Code*, a director or officer may be liable for trading in the corporation's securities with knowledge of confidential information that might reasonably be expected to affect materially the value of any of the securities.

Liabilities Specific to Public Corporations

[263] Directors of public corporations can be held liable for:

- incorrect information (written or oral) distributed by the corporation to the public;
- failure to comply with continuous disclosure requirements; and
- failure to file certain documents, such as financial statements, or for misrepresentations in such documents.

Directors may be held liable in civil, administrative quasi-criminal or criminal proceedings.

Liabilities Specific to Cannabis Industry

[264] Canadian federal and provincial cannabis legislation imposes liability on directors and officers of corporations if they directed, authorized, assented to, acquiesced in or participated in the commission of a violation of such legislation. The *Cannabis Act* (Canada) has expressly removed the ability of a director or officer to invoke a 'due diligence' or 'mistake of fact' defence. By contrast, the Ontario *Cannabis Control Act, 2017* has not expressly removed the availability of these defences.

2.6.11 Indemnification and Insurance

[265] Apart from the diligent discharge of their duties, there are a number of ways that directors and officers can manage the risks associated with their personal liability.

[266] A unanimous shareholder agreement can be used to shift some or all of the directors' responsibilities and liabilities to the shareholders of a corporation. Trust accounts and letters of credit can also be set up to ensure that the corporation does not default on payment of sums for which the directors and officers are personally liable. As well, resignation can protect directors and officers from liability for any events that occur subsequent to such resignation.

[267] A corporation may also indemnify its directors and officers (and others) who act at its request against all costs, including amounts paid to settle an action or satisfy a judgment. The preconditions to indemnification are: (1) the director or officer acted honestly and in good faith with a view to the best interests of the corporation; and (2) in the case of a criminal or administrative action or proceeding that is enforced by a monetary penalty, the director or officer had reasonable grounds for believing that the individual's conduct was lawful.

[268] Under the CBCA, indemnification may be provided for any civil or regulatory proceeding as well as with respect to criminal matters. The corporation may provide an advancement of indemnification prior to the conclusion of the proceeding. However, in the case of a derivative action, approval of the court is required prior to indemnification or advancement.

[269] A corporation may purchase and maintain insurance for its directors and officers. Directors and officers liability insurance ('D&O insurance') is widely available and it is advisable for directors and officers to have such insurance before agreeing to appointment to these positions. In the context of an M&A transaction resulting in a change of control of the target, special attention will be paid to ensuring that directors and officers have sufficient insurance coverage and rights to continuing indemnification. It is common for the target company to refresh or document the director's right to indemnification in a contract. This formal indemnity will generally also set out the company's obligation to ensure that adequate D&O insurance is maintained while the director or officer remains in that position and subsequently. This is because a director or officer may be subject to liabilities or exposure for alleged negligence or breach of fiduciary duty after the director or officer ceases to hold that position. Since D&O insurance is almost invariably on a 'claims made' basis, it is essential that there be adequate insurance for the duration of exposure to these liabilities. By ensuring that the target contractually agrees to maintain insurance and to indemnify the directors and officers, the target's outgoing directors and officers mitigate the possibility that the acquirer will change the indemnification and insurance arrangements to the detriment of the target's outgoing directors and officers.

[270] While insurance provides important protection, there are many exclusions from typical insurance policies, including:

- actions involving fraud, conspiracy, criminal acts, human rights violations or other intentional acts;
- the obtaining of a personal profit or advantage to which the recipient was not legally entitled;
- claims arising out of statutory liabilities;
- claims against a director by an insured under the same policy;
- claims for fines or penalties imposed by law, punitive or exemplary damages; and
- matters that the law may determine to be uninsurable.

As well, for some corporations, the premiums for such policies may be prohibitive.

2.6.12 Role of Shareholders in the Corporation

[271] Unless otherwise prescribed in the articles, by-laws or a unanimous shareholders agreement, shareholders have: (a) the right to vote on matters to be decided at shareholders meetings, (b) the right to participate in the distribution of profits by way of dividends, (c) the right to transfer his or her shares, and (d) the right to participate in the distribution of assets upon dissolution after payment of all of the corporation's liabilities. Shareholders do not, however, have the right to exercise control over the management of the corporation except through the election of a board of directors, except in the case of a unanimous shareholders agreement.

2.6.13 Limited Liability

[272] CBCA corporations limit the liability of shareholders to third parties. A shareholder is not entitled to a return of capital until all of the corporation's debts are paid. However, a shareholder is not liable for the debts, liabilities and obligations of the corporation except in a limited number of cases. These exceptions include:

- amounts received for improper reductions in stated capital;
- obligations assumed pursuant to a unanimous shareholders agreement; and
- improper distributions made upon dissolution.

The court retains the discretion to 'pierce the corporate veil' to impose liability on shareholders or parent companies. However, apart from the oppression remedy described below, this typically occurs only where the corporation has been used for a fraudulent purpose or it is clear that the corporation has been used solely as the alter ego of the shareholder and fairness requires that the corporate form be ignored.

2.6.14 Unlimited Liability

[273] As discussed previously, Nova Scotia, Alberta and British Columbia permit the incorporation of companies with unlimited shareholder liability. These unlimited liability companies can provide for beneficial US tax treatment in certain cross-border structures because such companies are treated as corporations under Canadian corporate and tax law but as disregarded entities for US tax purposes. However, such cross-border structures should be analysed from a tax perspective to assess whether any treaty benefits may be available.

2.6.15 Shareholder Meetings

[274] Decisions made by the shareholders of the corporation are made at shareholder meetings. There are four circumstances in which shareholder meetings must be called. Directors must call an annual meeting (as described below). Second, if there is any business that must be dealt with by way of a shareholders' resolution under the CBCA or the by-laws of the corporation, the directors must call a special meeting. Third, shareholders holding not less than 5% of the issued shares of the corporation carrying the right to vote may requisition the directors to call a meeting for the business set out in the resolution. Finally, the court may requisition a meeting upon an application of a director, shareholder or other proper party. The directors may fix the place for the meeting, subject to the by-laws. However, a shareholders' meeting must take place within Canada unless all of the shareholders agree or the articles provide for a place outside of Canada. In the case of public companies (reporting issuers), such companies are required to circulate an information circular and form of proxy soliciting votes with respect to the matters placed before the meeting.

Types of Meetings

[275] A CBCA company must hold its first annual meeting within eighteen months of incorporation and, thereafter, at least every fifteen months and within six months of the end of the corporation's fiscal year. There are three purposes to an annual meeting: (1) elect the directors; (2) receive financial statements and the auditor's report; and (3) appoint the auditor.

[276] A special meeting of shareholders may be held at any time (including, commonly, along with the annual meeting) in order to conduct business other than the business to be conducted at an annual meeting.

Record Date and Calling the Meeting

[277] Except in the case of a requisitioned meeting, the directors will pass a resolution calling a meeting. The directors may fix a record date establishing the list of the holders of shares entitled to receive notice of and to participate in the shareholders' meeting. Under the CBCA if a record date is not set, it will be deemed to be the close of business on the day immediately preceding the day on which notice is given. If a record date is set, the record date must not be less than twenty-one days and not more than sixty days prior to the date of the meeting. Reporting issuers using the notice-and-access system, which streamlines the process of distributing meeting materials to shareholders, must set a record date for notice that is not less than forty days before the date of the meeting. Notice must be given in writing to every shareholder entitled to vote, as well as every director and auditor of the corporation.

Quorum

[278] Typically, the quorum for the meeting will be described in the by-laws of the corporation. If no quorum is specified, then it is the holders of a majority of the shares entitled to vote at the meeting who are present in person or represented by proxy. However, the by-laws of most corporations specify a much smaller number.

Shareholder Proposals

[279] Shareholders holding 1% of the total number of the outstanding voting shares of the corporation or holding shares whose fair market value is at least CAD2 000 may submit a proposal for consideration at a shareholders' meeting. The directors of the corporation must include the proposal in the management proxy circular distributed in connection with the meeting or attach to it a statement in support of the proposal by the person and the name and address of the person. The proposal may include nominations for elections of directors provided that the proposal is signed by one or more holders of not less than 5% of the shares entitled to vote on the election of directors. However, it should be noted that shareholders may also nominate directors at the shareholders' meeting.

Proxy Solicitation

[280] Shareholders may vote by proxy. There are detailed rules regarding the form of proxies and the manner of their solicitation. Public corporations and corporations with more than fifty shareholders must deliver a management information circular and form of proxy. There are detailed requirements for the form and content of the proxy and the management information circular.

2.6.16 Voting Agreements

[281] Shareholders may contractually agree with each other to vote their shares in a certain way. However, voting agreements cannot fetter the discretion of the directors to act in the best interest of the company. Instead, shareholders may enter into a unanimous shareholders agreement to transfer decision-making powers to the shareholders (or some of the shareholders) so that the shareholders can make those decisions. In doing so, shareholders will take on the relevant directors' liabilities.

2.6.17 Fundamental Changes

[282] Certain fundamental changes to a corporation require approval by a special resolution of shareholders at a special meeting of shareholders. A special resolution under the CBCA is a resolution that is approved by a majority of not less than two-thirds of the votes cast by the shareholders who voted in respect of that resolution.

The following changes are considered to be fundamental changes:

- amendments to the articles of the corporation;
- the lease, exchange of all or substantially all of the assets of the corporation;
- continuance of the corporation to another jurisdiction;
- liquidation or dissolution of the corporation; and
- certain changes to stated capital.

Amendments to the Articles

[283] The requirement for a special resolution in respect of amendments to the articles will govern the following (among others):

- a change in name;
- a change to the province in which the registered office is located;
- the addition, change or removal of any restriction on the business or businesses that the corporation may carry on;
- a change to any maximum number of shares that the corporation is authorized to issue;
- the creation of new classes of shares;

- adding, changing or removing any rights, privileges, restrictions and conditions, including rights to accrued dividends, in respect of all or any of its shares, whether issued or unissued;
- changing the shares of any class or series, whether issued or unissued, into a different number of shares of the same class or series or into the same or a different number of shares of other classes or series;
- dividing a class of shares, whether issued or unissued, into series and fixing the number of shares in each series and the rights, privileges, restrictions and conditions thereof;
- increasing or decreasing the minimum or maximum number of directors; and
- adding, changing or removing restrictions on the issue, transfer or ownership of shares.

Sale of All or Substantially All of the Assets

[284] The question of whether a sale, lease or exchange involves all or substantially all of the assets of a corporation involves a quantitative test and a qualitative test. There is no bright line to guide the directors. However, typically the disposition, lease or exchange of more than 70% of the assets of the corporation by value is considered to be a sale of substantially all of the corporation's assets unless the corporation obtains legal advice to support a contrary conclusion. The qualitative test involves analysing whether the sale, lease or exchange of assets would fundamentally change the nature of the corporation or its business. If it would, then the sale requires the approval of the shareholders.

Dissent and Appraisal Rights

[285] Shareholders have dissent and appraisal rights for certain fundamental changes, such as a change to the articles. The dissent and appraisal right is only available to registered holders. The dissenting shareholder must strictly comply with the dissent procedures under the CBCA. This involves, among other things, providing the corporation with notice of the shareholder's intention to dissent and delivering up the shares issued to the shareholder following notice by the corporation that the resolution from which the shareholder dissents has become effective. The dissenting shareholder is entitled to be paid the fair value of the shareholder's shares as determined as of the close of business on the day before the resolution was adopted.

2.6.18 Derivative Actions and the Oppression Remedy

[286] Canadian business corporations law provides for two general mechanisms to redress governance of a corporation – the derivative action and the oppression remedy.

Derivative Actions

[287] A derivative action is an action that is brought in the name of and on behalf of the corporation by a shareholder or other proper complainant to assert a right of the corporation. The derivative action is, for example, the method by which a shareholder or other proper complainant may seek redress for a director's breach of the duty of loyalty, which is owed to the corporation.

A derivative action requires leave of the court. Typically, the threshold for leave is low and is satisfied where the following conditions are met:

(1) the complainant is:
  (a) a registered holder or beneficial owner or a former registered holder or beneficial owner of a security (which includes a debt obligation) of the corporation or any of its affiliates;
  (b) a director or an officer or a former director or officer of a corporation or any of its affiliates;
  (c) the Director appointed under the CBCA; or
  (d) any other person who, in the discretion of a court, is a proper person to make an application.
(2) the complainant has given at least fourteen days' notice to the directors of the corporation or its subsidiary of the complainant's intention to apply to the court for leave and the directors have refused or failed to bring the action;
(3) the complainant is acting in good faith; and
(4) it appears to be in the interests of the corporation or its subsidiary that the action be brought.

[288] A derivative action may proceed notwithstanding the majority of the shareholders have approved of the actions that are being complained of in the action. This prevents a majority shareholder from approving conduct that would otherwise be improper and to the detriment of the corporation. A derivative action cannot be settled without court approval.

Oppression Remedy

[289] The 'oppression remedy' is a statutory innovation in Canadian corporate law without direct analogues in other jurisdictions. The same class of complainants who may seek leave to bring a derivative action may also seek a remedy from the court where in respect of a corporation or any of its affiliates:

(a) any act or omission of the corporation or any of its affiliates effects a result;
(b) the business or affairs of the corporation or any of its affiliates are or have been carried on or conducted in a manner; or
(c) the powers of the directors of the corporation or any of its affiliates are or have been exercised in a manner, that is oppressive or unfairly prejudicial to or that unfairly disregards the interests of any security holder, creditor, director or officer.

[290] The oppression remedy has proven to be the main tool for challenging corporate conduct that is contrary to the reasonable expectations of security holders and creditors. The oppression remedy permits the court to enforce not only what is legal but also what is fair in the context of the reasonable expectations of stakeholders. In determining whether a reasonable expectation has been harmed by the conduct complained of in an oppressive or unfair way, the court will examine the nature of the corporation, the history of the relationships with the complaining stakeholders, general commercial practice, steps the claimant could have taken to protect itself, any representations or agreements relating to the issue, and the range of fair resolutions of conflicting interests between stakeholders.

2.6.19 Choice of Law and Forum Selection

[291] Canadian courts will enforce choice of law and forum selection clauses in contracts. It is feasible, and preferred, to subject contractual arrangements to the law of the province whose courts will have jurisdiction over the matter. This is because the application of foreign law must be proven as a question of fact (often using expert evidence) whereas this is not required for application of domestic law.

[292] Arbitration agreements are also presumptively enforceable and all Canadian provinces have adopted the UNCITRAL Model Law on International Commercial Arbitration. Courts are very receptive to enforcing an agreement to arbitrate. The inclusions of arbitration provisions are common and there are numerous well-qualified and experienced arbitrators to choose from in Canada.

2.6.20 Insolvency

[293] Canadian insolvency law is complex. There are many different types of proceedings that a debtor may be involved in. However, for the purposes of this section, there are two types of insolvency regimes that are relevant to mergers and acquisitions in Canada.

[294] The first type of regime is a reorganization proceeding which may be commenced pursuant to the CCAA or the BIA (typically used for smaller companies). The principal purpose of these proceedings is to provide a corporation with an opportunity to develop a plan or proposal for the continued existence of the corporation's business. The outcome of these proceedings is typically the compromise of existing claims of creditors and may also include a new entity taking over all or part of the corporation's business while any remaining parts are liquidated.

[295] The second type of regime is the liquidation of the company's assets. This can proceed within a CCAA proceeding; however, traditionally a pure liquidation process will occur within a bankruptcy proceeding under the BIA in which a trustee in bankruptcy takes possession and control of the assets of the debtor corporation for the benefit of all of the creditors. Liquidation may also occur under the BIA pursuant to a receivership proceeding initiated by a secured creditor.

Restructuring/Reorganization Proceedings

CCAA

[296] A debtor corporation or group of affiliated debtor corporations may apply for protection under the CCAA if the debtor corporation (a) is insolvent and (b) has at least CAD5 m of indebtedness. The first step is for the debtor corporation to bring an application before the court to obtain an 'Initial Order'. The Initial Order typically grants protection to the debtor corporation from its creditors by staying all proceedings against the debtor. On an initial application, the stay of proceedings may not exceed ten days; however, the stay is typically extended by subsequent court orders. The debtor corporation remains in possession and control of its assets subject to any orders made by the court. The Initial Order will also appoint a 'Monitor' (typically one of the accounting firms with expertise in corporate restructuring) to review the operations of the corporation during CCAA protection and to report to the court and creditors on the corporation's activities. The Monitor is an officer of the court and its advice to the court carries significant weight.

[297] A CCAA proceeding may be very lengthy. The primary purpose of a CCAA proceeding is to allow a debtor corporation to develop a plan of arrangement or compromise with its creditors to permit it to continue operations. This may involve significant negotiation to ensure that the plan has sufficient support. In addition, the debtor corporation may engage in sales of its business or assets that are not core to the restructured entity. The debtor corporation frequently requires time to renegotiate key contracts and seek concessions from employees. In some cases, the CCAA process turns into the liquidation of the entire enterprise.

[298] Any plan proposed by a debtor to its creditors must be approved by a majority in number representing two-thirds in value of the creditors, or the class of creditors, as applicable. The plan must also be sanctioned by the court.

BIA Proposal Proceedings

[299] A debtor company that is insolvent may commence a proposal proceeding pursuant to the BIA by filing a proposal or a notice of intention to make a proposal with the official receiver. The BIA proposal regime is less flexible than the CCAA and is typically utilized by smaller companies seeking to restructure their affairs. The purpose of the regime is to provide the debtor company with time to put forward a proposal to its creditors that will compromise their claims and result in the company's continued operations. A stay of proceedings is automatically imposed upon the filing of a proposal or a notice of intention to make a proposal. The initial stay upon the filing of a notice of intention to make a proposal is thirty days. The Court can grant extensions of the stay in forty-five-day increments for an additional five months after the expiration of the initial thirty-day period. Cumulatively, the total stay period from the date of filing the notice of intention cannot exceed six months. If a company does not file a proposal by the end of the stay period, the company is deemed to have made an assignment in bankruptcy. A proposal will only be approved by the requisite majority of creditors if it provides greater value to the company's creditors than a straight bankruptcy and liquidation of the company.

Bankruptcy Proceedings

[300] A bankruptcy proceeding pursuant to the BIA may be voluntary or involuntary.

[301] A voluntary proceeding is commenced by the debtor corporation following a resolution by the board of directors to assign the company into bankruptcy. The corporation files a prescribed form and a copy of the board resolution with the Official Receiver. The Official Receiver is the representative of the Superintendent of Bankruptcy of the federal government administration.

[302] An involuntary proceeding is commenced by a creditor who is owed CAD1 000 or more on an unsecured basis and initiates an application to have the debtor corporation adjudged bankrupt. In order to succeed, the debtor corporation must have committed an act of bankruptcy in the preceding six months. Acts of bankruptcy include, among other things:

- giving notice to the corporation's creditors that it has suspended or that it is about to suspend payment of the corporation's debts;
- ceasing to meet liabilities generally as they become due;
- exhibiting to a meeting of creditors any statement of its assets and liabilities that shows that the debtor corporation is insolvent, or presenting or causing to be presented to a meeting of creditors a written admission of the debtor corporation's inability to pay its debts; and
- making an assignment of property to a trustee for the benefit of creditors.

[303] Upon bankruptcy, a debtor corporation no longer has the ability to dispose of its property or otherwise deal with its assets. Instead, the property of the debtor corporation immediately vests in a trustee in bankruptcy, subject to the rights of secured creditors. The trustee in bankruptcy administers the estate, liquidates the debtor's assets and distributes the proceeds to the debtor's creditors in accordance with their respective priorities.

Receiverships

[304] Receivership proceedings are most frequently commenced by secured creditors seeking to enforce their security interest over collateral. There are two types of receiverships – court-appointed and private.

[305] Pursuant to the BIA, a court may appoint a receiver on an application by a secured creditor, if it is 'just and convenient' to do so. In Ontario, receivers are typically appointed both under the BIA and the provincial *Rules of Civil Procedure*. A court-appointed receiver is an officer of the court and will act on behalf of all creditors. Typically, the court-appointed receiver will administer a sale process and will report to and seek the approval of the court for a sale of the assets subject to the receivership order.

[306] A privately appointed receiver is appointed by a secured creditor pursuant to contractual rights in the security agreement with the debtor company. A privately appointed receiver is an agent of the secured creditor and will generally only act on behalf of the secured creditor that appointed them for the purpose of taking possession of the secured creditor's collateral, selling the collateral and distributing the proceeds to the secured creditor.

2.7 Specific Rules on Public Takeovers

[307] Securities of publicly traded companies are provincially regulated in Canada under the authority of the applicable securities commission. The provincial securities laws are harmonized across the different provinces and set out general requirements for public takeovers. These general requirements can be found in National Instrument 62-104 *Take-Over Bids and Issuer Bids*. In addition, some provinces have adopted specific requirements for takeover bids launched by an insider of the reporting issuer. Compliance with these requirements may be enforced by the courts or the securities commissions in each province.

[308] It should be noted that acquisitions beyond certain prescribed thresholds may trigger additional obligations for notification and review under the *Competition Act* and the *Investment Canada Act*. A buyer should take these regulatory requirements into consideration, particularly with respect to notification timelines, prior to launching a takeover bid.

2.7.1 Takeover Bid Defined

[309] A 'takeover bid' is an offer to purchase, from one or more security holders of the target company, at least one of which is located in Canada or has a Canadian address on the books and records of the reporting issuer, outstanding voting securities or equity securities of a class that together with the offeror's existing holdings and others acting jointly or in concert with the offeror, constitute in the aggregate 20% or more of the outstanding securities of the class being purchased. With few exceptions, once the 20% threshold is reached, an offeror must extend the offer to all security holders of the class, under a set of structured rules. It should be noted that there are certain exemptions (such as foreign takeover exemptions where fewer than 10% of the shareholders are Canadian) that allow a purchaser to acquire shares without triggering the obligations of the takeover regulations.

[310] In the case of friendly takeover bids, the offeror and the target company may agree to certain conditions, including a break fee, before the bid is officially issued in order to facilitate the transaction.

2.7.2 Early Warning

[311] Not uncommonly a potential offeror wishes to obtain a toehold in the target company before launching a takeover bid; in such cases, a potential offeror must be careful to abide by early warning disclosure requirements. The early warning disclosure threshold is reached when a person or entity acquires beneficial ownership of or the power to exercise control or direction over voting or equity securities that constitute in the aggregate 10% or more of the voting or equity securities of any class.

[312] A security holder that has made an early warning report (the 'acquirer') must make further disclosure each time the acquirer or any person or company acting 'jointly or in concert' with the acquirer acquires beneficial ownership of or the power to exercise control or direction over an additional 2% of the outstanding securities of or securities convertible into the same class to which the disclosure related. In addition, such security holders must disclose a change in any material fact in any previous early warning disclosure. Recent amendments to the early warning system require the security holder to also disclose decreases in ownership, control or direction of 2% or more of the outstanding securities of the applicable class and to disclose when their overall ownership, control or direction falls below 10%, which is often referred to as an 'exit report'.

[313] An offeror is defined to include any person acting 'jointly or in concert' with an offeror. An affiliate of an offeror is *deemed* to be acting jointly or in concert with the offeror. A person or company is also *deemed* to be acting jointly or in concert with the offeror if that person or company has an agreement, commitment or understanding with an offeror or any person acting jointly or in concert with the offeror under which the person acquires or offers to acquire securities of the same class as are subject to the offer. A person or company is *presumed* to be acting jointly or in concert with the offeror if that person or company has an agreement, commitment or understanding with an offeror or any person acting jointly or in concert with the offeror to vote the securities jointly and in concert with the securities of the same class as are subject to the offer. An associate of the offeror is also *presumed* to be acting jointly or in concert with the offeror. Importantly, an agreement to tender securities to a takeover bid or vote in favour of a transaction at a shareholder meeting will not, on its own, result in a person being deemed or presumed to be acting jointly or in concert with an offeror or acquirer.

[314] If the early warning obligations are triggered, the security holder acquiring or disposing of shares is required to issue and file a news release immediately and to file an early warning report within two business days following the acquisition or disposition. The security holder and any joint actors are prohibited from acquiring securities between the time of the triggering event and the end of the first full business day after the filing of the early warning report. The early warning report requires disclosure of information that is relevant to the ownership, control or direction over the securities including, but not limited to, the price paid, the purpose of the transaction, future intentions to acquire securities and descriptions of any agreements with joint actors.

2.7.3 Launching the Takeover Bid

[315] An offeror may commence a formal takeover bid in two ways. The offeror may publish an advertisement containing a brief summary of the bid in at least one major daily newspaper of general and regular paid circulation in Ontario. This is typically the method of commencing a non-consensual or 'hostile' takeover bid. The second method, more common in consensual arrangements, is for the offeror to send the bid to the target's security holders. In either case, the commencement of the bid will be followed by sending the bid, the takeover bid circular (discussed below) and any notices of change or variation to each shareholder.

[316] Securities laws impose a 50% minimum tender condition, which requires that more than 50% of the outstanding securities of the class subject to the bid be tendered in order for the bid to comply with takeover laws. The purpose of this requirement is to ensure that a change of control only occurs if it is supported by a majority of shareholders. It is still possible for a buyer to make a partial offer (for less than all of the outstanding shares), but this bid must be greater than 50% of the outstanding shares in the class.

2.7.4 Consideration for the Takeover Bid

[317] The consideration for the offer may involve cash, securities in the offeror or any other entity, or any combination of the foregoing. For example, an offeror could offer a mix of cash, securities in the offeror and securities in an affiliate of the offeror as consideration for the offer.

2.7.5 Pre-bid Integration

[318] Purchases made by the offeror within ninety days prior to the takeover bid may affect the consideration being offered in the takeover bid as a result of the application of pre-bid integration rules. These set a floor with respect to the value of the consideration that can be offered and may, in addition, constrain an offeror with respect to the mix of consideration that can be offered if the offer is not all cash. If the pre-bid integration rules apply (discussed below), then the offeror must offer to acquire at least the percentage of outstanding securities that is equal to the highest percentage of a seller's securities of that class in a transaction to which the pre-integration rules apply, and the offeror must offer:

- consideration that is at least equal to and in the same form as the highest consideration that was paid on a per security basis in a transaction to which the pre-bid integration rules apply; or
- consideration that is at least the cash value of the foregoing.

The pre-bid integration rules apply if, in the ninety days preceding the takeover bid, the offeror, or any person acting jointly or in concert with the offeror, acquired beneficial ownership of securities of the class that is the subject of the bid in a transaction not generally available on identical terms to all security holders of that class.

The pre-bid integration rules do not apply to trades in a security of an issuer that had not been previously issued or that had been issued and subsequently re-acquired by the issuer, or trades made in the normal course on an established market and:

- any broker acting for the offeror performs only the customary broker's functions in regard to the purchases and receives only the fees or commissions that are usual for comparable transactions in the normal course;
- the offeror or any person or company acting for the offeror does not solicit or arrange for the solicitation of offers to sell securities of the class subject to the bid; and

- the seller or any person or company acting for the seller does not solicit or arrange for the solicitation of offers to buy securities of the class subject to the bid.

[319] Exemptions from the takeover bid rules allow certain acquisitions that are technically takeover bids to occur without triggering the formal bid requirements. For example, under the 'private agreement' exemption, an offeror may acquire shares under a private agreement from, at most, five individuals or entities where the value of consideration paid for the securities is not greater than 115% of the 'market price' of the securities.

2.7.6 Equal Treatment

[320] An offeror must offer identical consideration to all holders of the securities that are the subject of the offer. In a conventional bid, the offeror will offer to purchase the securities for a specified cash consideration, share consideration or mix of cash and shares. The only decision that the security holder must make is whether or not to tender to the bid. The identical consideration rule does not, however, prevent the offeror from offering two or more alternative packages of consideration to security holders so long as the choice of consideration is provided to all holders of securities that are the subject of the offer. If the offeror increases the value of the consideration prior to the expiry of the bid, the offeror must pay that increased consideration to every security holder who deposited to the bid, irrespective of whether the security holder deposited prior to the notice of variation to the consideration.

2.7.7 Collateral Benefits Prohibited

[321] A corollary of the equal treatment rule is that there is a prohibition on providing direct or indirect collateral benefits to individual security holders or groups of security holders. An offeror who makes a bid or who intends to make a bid is prohibited from entering into an agreement, commitment or understanding that has the direct or indirect effect of providing a security holder with consideration that is of greater value than that offered to other security holders. Typical forms of collateral benefit include:

- additional or different consideration to a major shareholder, such as an agreement to enter into a secondary transaction that would preserve tax benefits for one shareholder that are not available to all shareholders;
- a commitment to acquire securities outside of a bid;
- forgiving a loan or a release of other liabilities of a shareholder or potential claims against that shareholder;
- a commitment to spin out assets to management or a shareholder or an understanding or commitment to explore such a possibility; and
- a commitment to do business with a shareholder or an understanding or commitment to explore such a possibility.

[322] In a consensual takeover bid, it is frequently the case that the offeror will seek to retain key employees and will, therefore, enter into agreements with those employees either prior to or during the bid. The prohibition on collateral benefits will not apply to employment benefits provided that certain criteria are met:

(1) the benefit is an enhancement to a group plan and the benefits provided by the plan are generally available to employees who hold positions of a similar nature; or
(2) the benefit is received as part of employment compensation, severance or other employment benefit arrangements, provided that:
   (a) the benefit is not conferred for the purpose of increasing consideration paid to the security holder as an incentive to deposit to the bid;
   (b) the benefit is not conditional on the security holder supporting the bid;
   (c) full particulars of the benefit are disclosed in the takeover bid circular or the director's circular; and either:
      - at the time of the announcement of the bid, the security holder and the associates of the security holder together own less than 1% of the class of securities that are the subject of the bid; or
      - an independent committee of the target company determines in good faith and discloses in the takeover bid circular or director's circular that the benefit is less than 5% of the consideration being received by the security holder under the offer, net of any costs to the security holder, after being advised by the security holder the amount of consideration that the security holder expects to receive.

2.7.8 Period of the Bid

[323] The rules relating to takeover bids are designed to facilitate auctions of the target. Amendments to the securities legislation that came into effect in 2016 increased the minimum bid periods, implemented a mandatory ten-day extension period and require at least 50% of outstanding shares to be tendered to a takeover bid in an effort to protect shareholders and provide the target company's management with an opportunity to effectively respond to an unsolicited takeover bid. Given this purpose, it is notable that friendly takeover bids may continue to be subject to the prior minimum period of thirty-five days.

[324] With some exceptions, the bid must be open for a minimum period of 105 days from the date the bid is commenced. It is also subject to a mandatory ten-day bid extension, which requires all non-exempt takeover bids to be extended for at least ten additional days after the bidder achieves the mandatory minimum tender condition and all other terms and conditions have been complied with or waived. This mandatory extension protects shareholders from being coerced into tendering their shares out of a concern that they will be left out and become a minority shareholder. The offeror is entitled to withdraw the bid after it has been made and most offers will be made subject to such withdrawal right.

[325] A bid expires at the later of:

- the end of the period, including any extension, that the offeror provides for the deposit; and
- the time at which the offeror becomes obligated by the terms of the bid to take up or reject the securities deposited under the bid.

[326] The offeror is not permitted to take up any shares until the expiry of the initial deposit period. An offeror has an obligation to take up securities deposited to the bid immediately following the expiry of the initial deposit period, assuming all other conditions have been satisfied, and pay for such securities within three business days of taking them up. Securities deposited during the mandatory ten-day extension period must be taken up and paid for within ten days of being deposited.

A security holder may withdraw any securities deposited to the bid at the later of:

- anytime before the securities have been taken up by the offeror;
- within ten days of a notice of change or of variation to the bid, subject to certain exceptions described below; or
- if the securities are not paid for by the offeror within three business days after the securities have been taken up.

2.7.9 Conditions to the Bid

[327] With the exception of bid financing conditions, an offeror has latitude in attaching conditions to the bid. Typically, an offeror whose goal is to acquire 100% of the target company will attach a condition that at least 90% of the outstanding securities of the class are deposited to the bid (in order to permit a squeeze-out transaction) or at least $66^{2/3}$% of the outstanding securities of the class are deposited to the bid (in order to ensure the ability to pass special resolutions).

Other common conditions include:

- satisfactory due diligence;
- regulatory approvals, if required, such as under the *Competition Act* or by an industry regulator such as the CRTC; and
- no material change in the business or affairs of the target company by the date that the bid expires or is taken up.

[328] If the bid consideration is all cash or part cash, the offeror must make adequate arrangements prior to commencing the bid to ensure that the required funds are available to pay for the securities that are the subject of the bid. However, the offeror's financing for the bid can have some conditionality so long as the offeror reasonably believes at the time of commencing the bid that the possibility is remote that the offeror will not be able to pay for the securities deposited to the bid, assuming any other conditions of the bid are satisfied or waived.

2.7.10 Disclosure by the Offeror

[329] The offeror and the directors of the target company each have disclosure obligations with respect to a takeover bid. This section addresses the duties of the offeror. The duties of the directors of the target company are described below.

[330] Irrespective of whether the takeover bid is commenced by way of a newspaper advertisement or delivery of the bid to the security holders, the offeror must prepare a takeover bid circular. If the takeover bid is commenced by a newspaper advertisement, the takeover bid circular must be delivered to the target company's principal office and filed on the target's SEDAR+ profile on or before the date of the first publication of the advertisement. In addition, the offeror must request a list of the security holders on or before the date of the advertisement and send the takeover bid circular to the security holders not later than two business days after the receipt of the list. If the bid is commenced by way of sending the offer to the security holders, the offeror must send a copy of the takeover bid circular to the target company and file it the same day that the bid is sent or as soon as is practicable afterwards.

[331] A takeover bid circular must contain certain prescribed information describing, among other things, the offeror, the bid, conditions to the bid and financing of the bid.

[332] If the consideration includes securities, the offeror must provide particulars of those securities, as well as the financial statements and other information required in a prospectus of the issuer of the securities being offered as consideration, including *pro forma* financial information prepared on the basis that the acquisition is completed.

[333] Advertising and public relations activities are allowed in the context of a bid. Once a takeover bid is launched, the offeror often retains a proxy solicitation or public relations firm to promote its position on the bid.

2.7.11 Directors' Circular

[334] The directors of the target also have an obligation to prepare a directors' circular, which must be sent to security holders and filed not later than fifteen days after the commencement of the bid. The directors of the target company have a duty to evaluate the terms of the bid. In addition to disclosing prescribed information, the directors' circular must:

- recommend to the security holders whether to accept or reject the bid and give reasons for the recommendation;
- state that the directors are unable to make or are not making a recommendation and state the reasons for being unable to make or not making a recommendation; or
- state that the directors are considering whether to make a recommendation to accept or to reject the bid, the reasons for not yet making the recommendation, and a caution not to deposit securities to the bid until further communication

from the directors, which must be sent at least seven days prior to the expiry of the bid.

[335] There is no legal requirement in Canada that the directors conduct an auction of the company in the context of a pending change of control, provided that, for corporate issuers, they act in the best interests of the company. In discharging this duty, the directors must have regard to considerations including the need to treat affected stakeholders (such as shareholders) in a fair manner. Other stakeholder groups include employees, suppliers, creditors, consumers, governments and the environment.

[336] In the event of a conflict among stakeholder interests, the directors are entitled to exercise their business judgment in good faith and on reasonable grounds in order to balance the competing interests and determine what is in the best interests of the corporation.

[337] Directors are also entitled to employ shareholder rights plans (SRP), also known as 'poison pills,' as defensive tactics against a hostile takeover bid. Generally, an SRP is designed to provide existing shareholders with the right to acquire additional shares upon the occurrence of certain events, which traditionally included an offer to acquire a percentage (e.g., 20%) of the corporation's shares of a particular class. The 2016 changes to the takeover bid rules mentioned above have significantly reduced the justification for, and in many cases the utility, of SRPs in Canada.

2.7.12 Obtaining the Balance of the Shares

[338] There are two mechanisms by which an offeror might acquire the balance of shares that are not tendered to the bid. First, if within 120 days of a takeover bid, the bid is accepted by the holders of not less than 90% of the shares of the class that are the subject of the bid, the offeror may engage in a compulsory acquisition or squeeze-out transaction. Shares already held by the offeror or on behalf of the offeror or an affiliate or associate of the offeror do not count for the purposes of determining whether the 90% threshold has been met.

[339] If the 90% threshold is met, the offeror may require the shareholders who have not tendered their shares to sell their shares at the same price as was offered under the takeover bid. Under the CBCA, the right to exercise the compulsory acquisition provisions must be exercised within 60 days of the termination of the takeover bid, and, in any event, within 180 days of the commencement of the takeover bid.

The right is exercised by delivering a notice to the non-tendering shareholders stating that:

- the shareholders holding not less than 90% of the shares of the class to which the takeover bid related tendered to the bid;
- the offeror is bound to take up and pay for or has taken up and paid for the shares tendered to the bid;
- the non-tendering shareholder must elect (a) to sell on the same terms as under the takeover bid or (b) dissent within twenty days and demand to be paid fair value;

- if the non-tendering shareholder fails to dissent within twenty days, then the non-tendering shareholder will be deemed to have accepted the consideration of the bid; and
- the non-tendering shareholder must deliver their shares to the company within twenty days after receiving the offeror's notice.

[340] The second way that an offeror may acquire the balance of the shares not tendered to the bid is through a second-step transaction. An offeror will utilize a second-step transaction if the offeror acquired fewer than 90% of the shares but at least the $66^{2}/_{3}$% necessary to approve a fundamental change in the nature of a going-private transaction. The transaction might take the form of a statutory arrangement in which the security holder is required to exchange any securities held for cash or securities in another entity.

2.8 Other Relevant Laws and Due Diligence Issues

2.8.1 Anti-corruption

[341] The *Criminal Code* contains five main offences relating to corruption and bribery committed in Canada. The offences are complex. The following is an overview and not a complete description of every possible way in which a bribery offence may take place:

- *Bribery of Judges or Members of Parliament or Provincial Legislative Assemblies*. Section 119 creates offences which apply to both the person who directly, or indirectly accepts a bribe and to the person who offers a bribe. The offence can be committed by making the offer, accepting, agreeing to accept or attempting to obtain a bribe. The offence can be committed even where the benefits of the bribe are to flow to another person. It is an element of the offences that the person offering or obtaining a bribe acts corruptly in that there is an attempt to influence the officeholder in his or her official capacity. This offence is an indictable offence with a maximum prison sentence of fourteen years.
- *Bribery of Police Officers or other Law Enforcement Officers*. This offence is similar to section 119, but the group of public officers is different. Section 120 addresses bribes to police officers, justices and others involved in the administration of the criminal law. There must be an intention to interfere with the administration of justice, procure or facilitate the commission of an offence or to protect an offender from detection or punishment. The person giving or receiving the bribe must act corruptly. This offence is an indictable offence with a maximum prison sentence of fourteen years.
- *Fraud on the Government (influence peddling)*. Section 121 creates a number of offences relating to fraud upon the government and is aimed at preventing influence peddling. The offences apply to the government official (or family member of the government official) and the person offering the bribe. The offence is committed if the act is done directly or indirectly. Among other prohibited acts, influence peddling can take the form of offering a loan or

benefits in order to obtain an advantage in government business or benefits which the government may confer. Section 121 also prohibits the attempted influencing of government tendering processes. This offence is an indictable offence with a maximum prison sentence of five years.

- *Municipal Officials*. Section 123 is aimed at municipal officials who seek out or accept benefits to be influenced and those who offer such benefits. The prohibited activities relate to efforts at influencing municipal officials in the performance of job-related responsibilities, including voting for a resolution, or doing (or not doing) an official act. This offence is an indictable offence with a maximum prison sentence of five years.
- *Giving or Receiving Secret Commissions (applies to private and public employees and agents)*. Section 426 describes the offence of giving secret commissions. A person who directly or indirectly corruptly gives, offers or agrees to give or offer to an agent, or who, being an agent, corruptly demands, accepts or offers or agrees to accept any reward, advantage or benefit of any kind in return for doing (or not doing) an act, or for showing favour or disfavour to another person, in relation to the business of his principal commits an indictable offence. The intent of section 426 is that no person shall make secret use of an agent's position and services by means of giving the agent any type of consideration for secret use of the agent's position and services. The maximum prison sentence for this offence is five years.

Typically, the consideration given in these offences will be defined as money, valuable consideration, office, place or employment. If the offence requires that the person act 'corruptly', the prosecutor must prove that the person offering the bribe was attempting to influence the person receiving the bribe to exercise his or her discretion or that the person receiving the bribe was receiving the bribe knowing that was the intention.

[342] Generally speaking, bribery and corruption offences under the *Criminal Code* are dual offences. In other words, they apply to both the person giving/offering the bribe as well as to the person accepting or agreeing to accept the bribe.

[343] Furthermore, bribery and corruption offences can be committed not only by the actual perpetrator of the offence but also by anyone who aids, encourages or counsels the actual perpetrators. This is known as the counselling offence and is found in section 22 of the *Criminal Code*. In addition, under section 24 of the *Criminal Code*, an attempt to commit a bribery or corruption offence is itself an offence.

Retaliation

[344] Under the *Criminal Code*, it is also an offence for a company to retaliate against an employee for reporting any of the above offences to the authorities. Section 425.1 makes it an offence for an employer or anyone acting on behalf of an employer to take or threaten to take disciplinary or other measures such as termination against an employee with the intent to compel the employee not to provide information to authorities whose duties include the enforcement of federal or provincial law respecting an offence that the employee believes has been or is being committed by the employer, an officer or employee of the employer or directors of a corporation. The maximum prison sentence for this offence is five years.

2.8.2 Corruption of Foreign Public Officials Act

[345] Amendments to the *Corruption of Foreign Public Officials Act* (CFPOA) made in 2013 provide Canadian authorities with the jurisdiction to pursue acts of bribery committed by any Canadian citizen, permanent resident or entity incorporated under the laws of Canada (or any province), no matter where in the world the act is alleged to have occurred and regardless of whether it has any connection to Canada.

[346] The CFPOA establishes two types of offences. First, it is a criminal offence for anyone to directly or indirectly give, offer, or agree to give or offer a corrupt benefit to a foreign public official or to any person for the benefit of a foreign public official in order to obtain or retain an advantage. A corrupt benefit includes a loan, reward, advantage or benefit of any kind. Second, it is an offence to create false books and records, or destroy such books and records, for the purpose of facilitating or hiding bribery of foreign officials. This is known as the accounting offence. The offences under the CFPOA are indictable offences each with a maximum prison sentence of fourteen years.

[347] Furthermore, the facilitation payments exception to the offence of bribing a foreign public official was repealed on 31 October 2017 by the Federal Government. Facilitation payments are payments made to foreign public officials for non-discretionary decisions that cover acts of a routine nature, for example, issuing business permits or licences. By repealing this exception, Canada became more closely aligned to the UK *Bribery Act* which does not allow for facilitation payments and moved away from the US *Foreign Corrupt Practices Act* which does allow for facilitation payments.

[348] Given the existence of a Canadian equivalent in the CFPOA, the UK *Bribery Act* and the US *Foreign Corrupt Practices Act*, representations and warranties regarding compliance with these statutes have become commonplace. It is also very common for acquirers to conduct extensive due diligence with respect to targets with subsidiaries in countries that are perceived to have a high risk for facilitation payments or other activities that could be an offence under these anti-corruption statutes. This is particularly the case for M&A transactions in the Canadian extractive resources sector.

2.8.3 Anti-money Laundering

[349] Canada enacted the *Proceeds of Crime (Money Laundering) Act* in 2000. This legislation was subsequently expanded to target terrorist financing and the legislation was renamed the *Proceeds of Crime (Money Laundering) and Terrorist Financing Act* (PCMLTFA).

[350] The PCMLTFA is primarily administered by the Financial Transactions and Reports Analysis Centre of Canada (FINTRAC). FINTRAC is an independent agency, at arm's length from law enforcement agencies, responsible for collecting, analysing and, in appropriate circumstances, disclosing certain limited information to law enforcement agencies.

[351] Reporting entities must implement a compliance programme, keep records and take steps to identify their clients. Reporting entities include:

- financial entities such as banks (those listed in Schedule I or II of the *Bank Act*) or authorized foreign banks with respect to their operations in Canada, credit unions, *caisses populaires*, financial services cooperatives, credit union centrals (when they offer financial services to anyone other than a member entity of the credit union central), trust companies, loan companies and agents of the Crown that accept deposit liabilities;
- life insurance companies, brokers and agents;
- securities dealers;
- money services businesses;
- agents of the Crown that sell money orders;
- accountants and accounting firms (when carrying out certain activities on behalf of their clients);
- real estate brokers, sales representatives and developers (when carrying out certain activities);
- mortgage administrators, brokers, and lenders;
- casinos;
- dealers in precious metals and stones; and
- public notaries and notary corporations of British Columbia (when carrying out certain activities on behalf of their clients).

Reporting entities must report transactions (including attempted transactions) if there are reasonable grounds to suspect that the transactions are related to the commission or attempted commission of a money laundering offence or a terrorist activity financing offence.

[352] Reporting entities have an obligation to report 'suspicious transactions' to FINTRAC. What used to be thirty days from the time the reporting entity 'first detects a fact that constitutes reasonable grounds to suspect' was in the 2019 amendment to the regulations of the PCMLTFA, changed to 'as soon as reasonably practicable' after the reporting entity has taken measures that enable them to establish that there are reasonable grounds to suspect that a transaction or attempted transaction is related to money laundering or terrorist financing. Further, reporting entities' obligations include reporting suspicious transactions or attempted suspicious transactions involving virtual currency.

[353] Reporting entities must also report large cash transaction reports to FINTRAC. Large cash transactions involve the receipt of CAD10 000 or more in cash in the course of a single transaction or in multiple transactions within a consecutive twenty-four hours by or on behalf of the same entity.

[354] Under the current regime, financial entities, money services businesses and casinos have to report incoming and outgoing international electronic funds transfers (EFT) of CAD10 000 or more in a single transaction or in multiple transactions within a consecutive twenty-four hours by or on behalf of the same entity The definition of EFT is no longer limited to cross-border transactions. Further, multiple transactions of less than CAD10 000 made over a twenty-four-hour period will be deemed to be a single transaction and would therefore be reportable, where the reporting entity knows that:

(1) For large cash or virtual currency transactions and EFTs initiated by a reporting entity:
   - the transactions are conducted or initiated by the same person or entity;
   - the transactions or requests are conducted or made on behalf of the same person or entity; or
   - the amounts are for the same beneficiary.

(2) For EFTs received by a reporting entity:
   - the EFTs are initiated at the request of the same person or entity; or
   - the amounts are for the same beneficiary.

(3) For casino disbursements:
   - the disbursements are requested by the same person or entity;
   - the disbursements are received by the same person or entity;
   - the disbursements are requested on behalf of the same person or entity; or
   - the disbursements are received on behalf of the same person or entity.

[355] Reporting entities must also report to FINTRAC if they have property in their possession or control that belongs to a terrorist group or a person listed under the Regulations Implementing the United Nations Resolutions on the Suppression of Terrorism.

[356] Failure to comply with the obligations to implement a compliance regime, make reports, keep records and confirm the identity of clients is punishable by administrative monetary penalties that can range up to CAD100 000 per violation for an individual and CAD500 000 per violation for a corporation. Non-compliance is also a criminal offence punishable by up to five years imprisonment, a fine of CAD500 000, or both. Failure to report suspicious transactions may be punishable by penalties up to CAD2 m and five years' imprisonment. Further amendments to the PCMLTFA recently came into effect in 2024, and one of the key highlights of the Act and associated regulations is the requirement for financial entities entering into a correspondent bank relationship to apply additional anti-money laundering and anti-terrorist financing standards. This is in view of the high level of vulnerability of most transactions requiring corresponding bank relationships. International trade-based financial crime has been seen as a major leverage for money launderers due to the potential for several layered transactions. The Federal Government continues to move forward with its ongoing plans to create the Canada Financial Crimes Agency. This Agency is to have the responsibility of investigating complex crimes and enforcing federal law, while consolidating on existing law enforcement resources of the Royal Canadian Mounted Police, FINTRAC, and the Canada Revenue Agency. The 2024 Budget notes the intention of the Federal Government to strengthen the powers of the Canada Border Services

Agency (CBSA) under the PCMLTFA by expanding its responsibilities and creating a Trade Transparency Unit within the CBSA to help combat financial crime. Plans to create a Market Watch Unit within the CBSA to facilitate trade remedy measures on an annual basis are also underway.

2.8.4 Environmental Regulations

[357] Federal and provincial governments have shared jurisdiction over environmental protection. A comprehensive review of Canadian environmental legislation with respect to the operation of a business in Canada goes beyond the scope of this section. However, Canadian environmental practices require special attention in mergers and acquisitions transactions because of the breadth of potential regulatory liability and the expense of legacy environmental issues.

[358] A corporation may be liable with respect to past environmental violations in connection with assets that have already been disposed. This should be borne in mind when conducting a share purchase transaction. It is not possible to contract out of potential regulatory liability. In an asset transaction, the purchaser will not be liable for violations except in respect of the specific assets acquired. A purchaser of assets would not be exposed to liability for violations that arose before the contamination; however, in the case of land, the purchaser will be liable for future remediation orders including contamination before purchase.

[359] Even lenders may be liable for environmental contamination if they become involved in the financial management of a corporation, the day-to-day operational management thereof, or if they become owners by way of foreclosure. However, there may be statutory exclusions for secured lenders, receivers and owners by foreclosure for certain aspects of liability.

Environmental Permits

[360] Canadian environmental law typically operates based on a 'permit' system, which prohibits the release of any substance into the environment that could cause 'an adverse effect'. An 'adverse effect' may include not only chemical discharges but also items such as dust, noise, light and vibration. This means that most industrial and manufacturing operations would require a permit, which, in Ontario, is called 'Environmental Compliance Approval' (ECA). The ECA will establish the maximum discharge quantities for the substance and will also impose conditions, including monitoring and reporting obligations. The ECA may also require the permit holder to provide financial assurances to secure decommissioning and rehabilitation costs.

[361] It is important to note that not all permits are assets that may be purchased or transferred to a new owner in an asset sale as of right. It may be necessary for the purchaser to make an application for a new ECA or permission to transfer. However, if there is no underlying change to the operations, such as the sale of a business and the transfer of associated personnel as a going concern, regulators may expedite the process.

Environmental Assessments

[362] Major new projects may require an environmental assessment before a permit may be obtained. In some cases, it may be necessary to conduct both a provincial and a federal environmental assessment. During the environmental assessment process, the proponent of the project will commission a comprehensive study of the project's environmental impact and will engage the public and, if required, aboriginal consultation.

2.8.5 Aboriginal Law and the Duty to Consult

[363] Canada's *Constitution Act, 1982* recognizes and affirms existing aboriginal and treaty rights of aboriginal peoples, which includes Canada's First Nations peoples, Inuit and Métis peoples. These aboriginal rights may include traditional rights to hunt, fish, trap and gather and the right to occupy and use land.

[364] Although much of Canada is subject to historical or modern treaties, which involved Canada's aboriginal peoples ceding certain rights to Canada, there are still broad swaths of Canada where there are unsettled claims.

[365] Federal and provincial governments have a legal duty to consult aboriginal peoples with respect to proposed conduct that may affect aboriginal rights, including development and activities on lands that are subject to land claims or treaty rights. If appropriate, federal and provincial governments must accommodate aboriginal communities. This 'duty to consult' may be delegated to the private sector proponent of a project, although ultimate consultation responsibility remains with the federal or provincial government.

[366] The duty to consult is triggered when the government has real or constructive knowledge of the potential existence of an aboriginal interest that may be adversely affected by an activity. The extent of consultation and accommodation varies with the type of project and is proportionate to the strength of the facts establishing the aboriginal right and the extent of the potential impairment. If there is inadequate consultation, the courts may enjoin further activity until there has been adequate consultation.

[367] In some cases, consultation may result in development frameworks with aboriginal groups in which the benefits of the project, including, for example, local employment and skills training, may be shared with the aboriginal groups.

2.8.6 Privacy Regulation & Government Information

[368] Canada's privacy laws fall into three categories: comprehensive private sector privacy laws, public sector privacy laws and sectoral laws, of which those regulating personal health information are the most relevant. In addition, Canadian governments, agencies, Crown corporations and other regulated entities, such as public hospitals, may be subject to access to information legislation. A detailed review of privacy and government information laws goes beyond the scope of this section. Instead, this section provides information that is relevant to issues that are specific to mergers and acquisitions.

Private Sector Privacy Legislation

[369] Canada's federal *Personal Information Protection and Electronic Documents Act* (PIPEDA) governs the collection, use, and disclosure of personal information of all private sector businesses in Canada. British Columbia, Alberta and Québec each have comprehensive private sector legislation that pre-empts PIPEDA (with an important exception) as a result of those laws being declared to be 'substantially similar' to PIPEDA. The exception to pre-emption is with respect to federal works, undertakings and businesses (FWUBs). FWUBs remain subject to PIPEDA. FWUBs include banks, airlines, interprovincial railways and other businesses that come within the exclusive regulatory jurisdiction of the federal government. This section focuses primarily on PIPEDA.

[370] PIPEDA defines personal information as information about an identifiable individual. Personal information excludes business contact information, such as names, positions, titles, work contact details and any other information used to communicate or facilitate communication with an individual about their employment, business or profession. It should be noted that it is unnecessary for a person's name to be associated with data in order for that data to be personal information. Provided that the data could be linked to other identifying data, the information will be considered 'personal' for the purposes of PIPEDA.

[371] PIPEDA imposes obligations on organizations that collect, use or disclose personal information in the course of commercial activities. In the case of FWUBs, PIPEDA also applies to information that is about an employee of the organization and that the organization collects, uses or discloses in connection with the operation of the FWUB. The private sector privacy legislation of British Columbia, Alberta and Québec also applies to employees. As a result, subject to limited exceptions, employees in those provinces have the same rights as other individuals when their personal information is collected, used or disclosed by their employer. However, in other provinces, such as Ontario, there is a legislative gap regarding employees' personal information since PIPEDA's application is limited to employment in federally regulated sectors. In those provinces, employees' privacy rights derive from common law, including those based on implied terms in an employment contract or express terms in a collective bargaining agreement.

[372] PIPEDA has a favourable partial 'adequacy' designation for the purposes of compliance with the EU General Data Protection Regulation (GDPR), which came into effect on 25 May 2018 (replacing the former Directive 95/46/EC). The 'adequacy' designation permits the free flow of personal data from the EU to Canada without the requirement for model clauses or other measures. However, the 'adequacy' designation only applies if the personal data is subject to PIPEDA. Since FWUBs form a minority of Canadian businesses with European operations, this means that most employee data transferred to Canada from the EU must comply with the restrictions in the GDPR. Since PIPEDA applies to non-employee data when transferred across borders, the adequacy ruling should apply to customer data even when that data is transferred to a province with its own privacy laws that apply instead of PIPEDA (i.e., Alberta, British Columbia and Quebec). Acquirers targeting Canadian businesses with material EU operations should conduct careful due diligence on whether the organization is compliant with applicable EU data protection obligations. Under the GDPR, the EU must assess the adequacy of PIPEDA's protection every four years. The latest adequacy decision was made on 15 January 2024.

[373] With some exceptions, PIPEDA requires that organizations obtain consent from individuals before collecting, using or disclosing their personal information. Such consent may be written or verbal, express or implied. Whether express ('opt-in') or implied ('opt-out') consent is required depends on the sensitivity of the personal information, the reasonable expectations of the individual and whether the collection, use or disclosure would create a meaningful residual risk of significant harm. The fact that the information is collected from a public source is not an exception to the consent requirements unless the public source is specifically recognized in a regulation made under PIPEDA. In practice, there are few public source exceptions available.

[374] Due diligence of corporations with significant data assets or customer lists should involve the review of privacy compliance. Organizations should have a Privacy Officer or equivalent person who is accountable for the organization's privacy practices. Attention should be paid to whether the personal information held by the organization was collected with consent, or based on a consent exception. Attention should also be paid to whether the organization is able to confirm that the purposes for which the organization uses and discloses the personal information – and the purposes contemplated by the acquirer – fall within the scope of that consent or consent exception. In addition, the acquirer in a share or asset purchase transaction will want to be satisfied that there are administrative, technical and physical security controls in place to protect the personal information from unauthorized access, use or disclosure. An acquirer should request information regarding any data breaches that the target company has experienced in recent history, the remediation efforts that ensued, and the results of any investigations. Consideration should also be given to indemnification provisions with respect to any personal information that the vendor will retain – in their systems or files – following an asset sale.

[375] PIPEDA includes a consent exception for the use and disclosure of personal information in the course of a business transaction, including in the due diligence phase. A business transaction is defined under PIPEDA to include the purchase, sale or other acquisition or disposition of an organization or any of its assets, the merger or amalgamation of organizations, and the lease or licensing of any of an organization's assets, among other things. This exception allows organizations to use and disclose personal information without consent in the context of a business transaction, so long as certain requirements are met. First, the parties to the transaction must have entered into an agreement that requires them to use and disclose the information solely for purposes related to the transaction, protect the information with adequate security safeguards, and return or destroy the information within a reasonable time if the transaction is not completed. Second, personal information must be necessary to determine whether to proceed with the transaction and to complete it.

[376] Once the transaction is completed, the personal information may continue to be used by the acquiring organization if the information is necessary for carrying on the business objective of the transaction and the individual whose information is being used is notified of the disclosure within a reasonable time after the transaction is completed.

[377] There must also be an agreement in place requiring both parties to only use and disclose the personal information without fresh consent for the purposes for which the information was originally collected and permitted to be used and disclosed, to protect the information, and to give effect to any withdrawals of consent. This consent exception does not apply to a business transaction whose primary purpose or result is the purchase, sale or other acquisition, disposition or lease of personal information.

[378] The privacy legislation of Alberta, British Columbia, and Quebec include similar business transaction exceptions. In the Alberta legislation, for example, a business transaction includes the purchase, sale, lease, merger or amalgamation or taking of a security interest in an organization or any business or activity or business asset of an organization. It also includes any prospective business transaction. Personal information may be collected, used and disclosed without consent as part of the transaction process if the use of the information is necessary for determining whether to proceed with the transaction and, if so, to complete it, the use is restricted to purposes related to the transaction and, if the transaction proceeds, to the purposes for which it was originally collected. As with PIPEDA, the parties must enter into an agreement to this effect. Alberta's legislation does not include a notice requirement like that seen in PIPEDA.

[379] Similarly, a business transaction under British Columbia's legislation means the purchase, sale, lease, merger, amalgamation or any other type of acquisition, disposal or financing of an organization. In British Columbia, an organization may disclose personal information about its employees, customers, directors, officers or shareholders without consent to a prospective party for purposes related to a proposed business transaction if the information is necessary to determine whether to proceed with the transaction. The parties must enter into an agreement restricting the use and disclosure of personal information for purposes related to the transaction. If the business transaction occurs, individuals must be notified that the business transaction has taken place and that personal information about them has been disclosed to the receiving party. Further, the receiving party may only use or disclose the personal information for the same purposes for which it was originally collected, used or disclosed. Under both Alberta and British Columbia's statutes, if a business transaction does not proceed, the prospective party must destroy or return any personal information to the organization. Similar to PIPEDA, the Alberta and British Columbia exceptions do not apply to business transactions where the primary purpose, objective or result of the transaction relates to the personal information itself. Under the Quebec private sector privacy law, an organization is permitted to disclose personal information without consent where it is necessary for concluding a commercial transaction. 'Commercial transaction' is defined as the 'alienation or leasing of all or part of an enterprise or of its assets, a modification of its legal structure by merger or otherwise, the obtaining of a loan or any other form of financing by the enterprise or of a security taken to guarantee any of its obligations'. To rely on this exception, the parties must enter into an agreement requiring the receiving party to only use the personal information for the purposes of concluding the transaction, not disclose the personal information without consent, protect the confidentiality of the personal information, and destroy the personal information if the transaction does not proceed or if the information is no longer necessary for completing the transaction. Within a reasonable time after the transaction is complete, the receiving party must notify individuals that it now holds the personal information about them.

[380] As of 1 November 2018, PIPEDA's mandatory breach reporting requirements are in force (Breach Notification Requirement). The Breach Notification Requirements oblige organizations subject to PIPEDA to report any 'breach of security safeguards' involving personal information under its control if it is reasonable to believe that the breach creates a 'real risk of significant harm' (RROSH) to an individual. A 'breach of security safeguards' is defined as 'a loss of, unauthorized access to or unauthorized disclosure of personal information'. Where the RROSH threshold is met, an organization must report the breach to the Office of the Privacy Commissioner of Canada (the OPC) and notify the affected individuals in accordance with the regulations. The Breach Notification Requirement is a significant privacy consideration for organizations subject to PIPEDA, as breach notifications can lead to class actions, regulatory investigations, and other civil actions and dispute resolution processes that might attach to the organization's overall liability. The privacy regimes in Alberta and Quebec have similar data breach reporting obligations. It is expected that British Columbia will amend its privacy statutes to also include mandatory breach reporting requirements in the near future.

[381] On 22 September 2021, Bill 64, *An Act to modernize legislative provisions as regards the protection of personal information,* received Royal Assent, significantly amending Quebec's private and public sector privacy legislation. Bill 64 introduced several amendments including significant administrative sanctions, data breach reporting obligations, rights relating to data portability and de-indexation, mandatory appointment of a privacy officer, and privacy impact assessment requirements. To comply with Bill 64, organizations have had to establish more robust data governance processes, develop corporate data management policies, and adopt technological solutions to de-index or transfer personal information upon request. Bill 64 has come into effect in three phases, with most provisions being in force as of 22 September 2023 (the final provisions will come into effect on 22 September 2024). Acquirers targeting businesses subject to Quebec's overhauled privacy legislation should conduct careful due diligence on whether the organization is compliant with the updated obligations.

Public Sector Privacy Laws

[382] Public sector privacy legislation has limited relevance to mergers and acquisition transactions. However, these laws may be relevant when acquiring businesses with significant public contracts.

[383] Nova Scotia's public sector privacy legislation requires that public bodies and their service providers ensure that personal information under their custody or control is stored and accessed only in Canada, subject to certain exceptions including the explicit consent of the individual.

[384] This legislation was enacted specifically to address the concerns of Canadians with respect to the potential application of the USA Patriot Act and the potential access by US law enforcement agencies to the personal information of Canadians.

[385] There are currently no statutory data residency requirements for personal information in the control of the federal government. As of 1 April 2020, the federal Policy on Service and Digital, Directive on Service and Digital (DSP), and Guideline on Service and Digital (the Guideline) have served as an integrated set of rules that articulate how Government of Canada organizations manage service delivery, information and data, information technology and cyber security. The DSP applies to departments as defined in section 2 of the *Financial Administration Act* unless otherwise excluded by other acts, regulations or orders in council. The DSP states that the Chief Information Officer of any department must identify and evaluate computing facilities located within Canada as the 'principal delivery option' for information categorized as Protected B, Protected C, or Classified (Classified data is data that, if compromised, would reasonably be expected to cause an injury to the national interest, and includes data that has regulatory or statutory prohibitions and controls. Protected B and Protected C data is data that, if compromised, could cause serious or extremely grave injury to an individual, organization or government). There are no data residency restrictions for unclassified information or information categorized as Protected A. The Guideline advises that the data residency policy applies to the *storage* of data, not the residency of data in transit. It also confirms that approved computing facilities need not be owned by Canadian corporations. In cases where a transaction or contract involves access to Protected B, Protected C, or Classified information, these data localization directions should be considered.

Personal Health Information Legislation

[386] Although Ontario does not have provincial privacy legislation governing the private sector, it has sectoral personal health information legislation, entitled the *Personal Health Information Protection Act* (PHIPA). Many other provinces have also enacted sectoral personal health information. In British Columbia and Alberta, the relevant requirements are largely incorporated into the public and private sector privacy legislation, with supplementary legislation or regulations dealing with electronic health records.

[387] In Ontario, PHIPA establishes the information practices for the collection, use, retention and disclosure of personal health information by 'health information custodians' and their service providers. Typically, a custodian is a health service provider, such as a physician, nurse, chiropractor, dentist, or a person who operates a health service facility, programme, or service, such as hospitals, long-term care homes, pharmacies, laboratories, ambulances, and community health centres.

[388] Acquirers of companies that are classified as health information custodians or their service providers should engage in a detailed review of the adequacy of the organization's personal health information practices during the due diligence process.

[389] Unlike private sector privacy legislation, PHIPA does not contain a business transaction exception for the use and disclosure of personal health information without consent during due diligence or on an asset sale.

Government Information

[390] Public institutions in Canada may be subject to access to information or freedom of information legislation, which provides individuals with a right of access to government records. Organizations conducting business with public institutions, such as municipalities and government ministries, must be aware that information (including information that organizations consider to be confidential) may be disclosed to requesters pursuant to these freedom of information regimes.

[391] For example, there are relatively narrow exceptions to the disclosure requirements under the federal *Access to Information Act*. If the record contains information about a third party, such as a tender document submitted by an organization in response to a Request for Proposals, the record must be disclosed to a requester unless it contains:

- trade secrets of a third party;
- financial, commercial, scientific or technical information that is confidential information supplied to a government institution by a third party and is treated consistently in a confidential manner by the third party;
- information that is supplied in confidence to a government institution by a third party for the preparation, maintenance, testing or implementation by the government institution of emergency management plans and that concerns the vulnerability of the third party's buildings or other structures, its networks or systems, including its computer or communications networks or systems, or the methods used to protect any of those buildings, structures, networks or systems;
- information the disclosure of which could reasonably be expected to result in material financial loss or gain to, or could reasonably be expected to prejudice the competitive position of, a third party; or
- information the disclosure of which could reasonably be expected to interfere with contractual or other negotiations of a third party.

These exemptions, and the corresponding ones under provincial legislation, have been interpreted narrowly. Of particular interest to third parties is the fact that a negotiated agreement (i.e., a contract) is typically not considered to be 'information supplied' to a government institution for the purposes of these exemptions, and as a result, those types of documents are often subject to disclosure requirements.

2.8.7 Anti-spam and Privacy

[392] Canada's Anti-Spam Legislation (CASL) came into force on 1 July 2014 and is one of the most robust anti-spam regimes in the world. This legislation has broad-reaching effects on the transmission of commercial electronic messages (CEM), as well as the installation of computer programs. With limited exceptions, the legislation requires express opt-in consent from the recipient of a CEM or the installation of a computer program.

Commercial Electronic Messages

[393] A CEM is an electronic message that encourages participation in a commercial activity. An electronic message may have a number of purposes, but so long as one of those purposes is to encourage a commercial activity, it will be considered a CEM under CASL. Among other things, a CEM can be transactional or promotional in character. With a few exceptions, a 'commercial activity' is defined as any transaction, act, conduct or regular course of conduct of a commercial character. It does not matter whether there is an expectation of profit. Whether a message is a CEM will be determined by taking account of the message as a whole including any hyperlinks in the message.

Consent Requirements and Exceptions for CEMs

[394] CASL applies to CEMs sent by or accessed from a computer system located in Canada. CASL prohibits sending (or causing or permitting the sending – e.g., by a marketer on behalf of an organization) CEMs to an 'electronic address' unless:

(i) the recipient expressly or impliedly consents *and* the message complies with the form and content requirements; or
(ii) an enumerated exception to the consent requirement applies.

[395] An 'electronic address' includes email, telephone, and instant messaging accounts, and any other similar accounts, which may include social media accounts. Websites and blogs are typically not considered to be electronic addresses.

[396] The default consent under CASL is express, or 'opt-in,' consent, which requires affirmative action on the part of the recipient. Express consent can be obtained orally or in writing. When obtaining express consent, the notice must clearly identify who is seeking consent, set out the purpose for which the consent is being sought, provide a mailing address and telephone number or email or web address of the organization seeking consent, and include a statement advising the individual that they can withdraw their consent at any time. All CEMs must include an unsubscribe mechanism that is quick and easy for the recipient to use if they wish to withdraw their consent.

Administrative Monetary Penalties

[399] The CRTC has the power to issue administrative monetary penalties for violations of CASL. The administrative monetary penalties for an organization could be as much as CAD10 m per violation. The CRTC engages in active enforcement and has entered into settlement agreements with several legitimate Canadian businesses. As of 2024, the CRTC's enforcement efforts have resulted in over CAD3.2 m in administrative monetary penalties.

Implications for M&A

[400] CASL has affected M&A in Canada in two main ways. First, acquirers of Canadian businesses have begun to engage in significant due diligence on customer lists and other data entered into customer relationship management systems to ensure that this valuable intellectual property can be used to legally communicate with customers. Failure to maintain records demonstrating CASL compliance may result in the inability to use customer contact information for CEMs, which may significantly impair the goodwill of the company. Second, in the context of an asset sale where customer lists and contact information are acquired pursuant to the sale, the acquiring company is generally permitted to rely on the express consents obtained by the seller as a basis for sending CEMs, as long as the other CASL requirements are met. However, the same may not be true when an acquiring company only purchases a customer list and contact information, and no other assets. As this issue is evolving, acquirers should seek legal advice before sending any CEMs to a target's customers.

[401] Finally, it is now common for organizations to seek representations and warranties from business partners and M&A targets that they have implemented governance programmes to comply with CASL and that they are complying with CASL. Violations of CASL compliance are often not governed by contractual limitations of liability.

2.9 The Due Diligence and Key Terms

[402] Sophisticated vendors and purchasers in the Canadian M&A market are familiar with the concept of a full due diligence investigation into various issues including commercial, financial, property, tax and environmental matters. The types of investigations pursued will depend on the nature of the acquisition. It is typical to conduct various corporate and security searches against the target corporation and to use 'data rooms' for the exchange of information between the parties. Environmental audits may be conducted where appropriate.

[403] Canadian courts favour the enforcement of contracts between commercial parties with a view to holding the parties to their bargains. The enforcement process and its duration will vary depending on the dispute at hand. To ensure the enforceability of key contractual provisions it is important that they are drafted clearly to capture the intentions of the parties. Special rules may apply to certain provisions such as non-compete covenants and these are further discussed in the 'Anti-competitive Restraints' and 'Retention of Key Personnel' sections.

2.9.1 Confidentiality Agreement

[404] Typically negotiations in Canada will begin with the parties entering into a confidentiality agreement to protect the confidential business information that will be shared in the course of exploring whether to pursue a deal. The confidentiality agreement will usually restrict the use of confidential information to the evaluation and negotiation of a purchase and sale transaction. Frequently, confidentiality agreements in private M&A transactions in Canada will also contain exclusivity provisions prohibiting the vendors from discussing alternative deals with third parties for a specified period of time.

[405] The vendor will usually want to obtain a broad all-encompassing definition of what is confidential. The confidentiality agreement will typically provide that any intellectual property that is shared will, notwithstanding having been shared, remain solely owned by and for the use of the disclosing party. The obligations to maintain confidentiality will generally be indefinite except with respect to information that becomes public other than by the action or negligence of the party receiving the confidential information.

[406] The receiving party will usually covenant to provide notice (unless prohibited by law) of any third party demand for access to the disclosing party's information (such as a governmental agency or in litigation). This obligation is important to the disclosing party to permit the disclosing party an opportunity to seek protective action.

2.9.2 Letter of Intent

[407] In Canada, it is also common for the potential vendor and purchaser to enter into a letter of intent or term sheet setting out the indicative terms for the transaction with the intention of negotiating a more formal agreement. Care must be taken with respect to the drafting of these documents because these documents may create binding obligations.

[408] In assessing whether a letter of intent or term sheet evidences a binding agreement, Canadian courts will review whether:

- the essential terms of the transaction are set out in the document or whether critical terms are missing and were to be negotiated as part of the subsequent formal agreement;
- the terms are vague or whether they are sufficiently clear and detailed to be enforced;
- the document uses contractual language signifying an intention to be bound; and
- the obligations are expressed to be conditional on satisfactory negotiation of the subsequent more formal agreement.

2.9.3 Purchase Price: Financing and Payment

[409] There are several possible ways in which a purchase price may be financed and paid:

- the vendor may finance the acquisition and take security over the shares or assets sold;
- an 'earn-out' arrangement may be used to adjust the final purchase price in accordance with a formula agreed to by the parties using the financial performance of the acquired business as of certain specified dates; or
- the purchase price may be paid out over time. Federal income tax legislation permits the vendor to take a reserve for amounts not paid to the vendor in the year of sale. The maximum period of deferral is five years for capital property and three years for non-capital property.

[410] Although often considered, 'earn-out' provisions also frequently lead to disputes among the vendor and purchaser over calculation. In addition to ensuring detailed metrics for financial performance, including detailed definitions of financial concepts, it is generally recommended that parties enter into a robust dispute resolution procedure. Care should be given to ensuring that an independent expert can be appointed to resolve disputes to avoid costly litigation. Notwithstanding the foregoing, note that in recent years, public-style deals have become more common in the Canadian M&A market whereby 'earn-out' arrangements are not utilized and terms are increasingly more vendor-friendly.

2.9.4 Representations and Warranties

[411] In a share purchase agreement, representations and warranties are particularly important in allocating risk and permitting the purchaser to make assumptions about the business being acquired. However, representations and warranties will be used in both asset and share transactions to create closing conditions (that the representations remain true) and the grounds for post-closing remedies (if it is determined subsequently that the representations were not true).

Disclosure Letters

[412] Part of the due diligence process in a share or asset transaction may be a disclosure letter from the vendor to the purchaser. The disclosure letter provides information about material issues that may become the subject of representations and warranties. For example, a disclosure letter may set out material contracts, known environmental liabilities, pension plans, and other information regarding the business. This permits the representations and warranties in a share or asset purchase agreement to be drafted in the negative with reference to the disclosure letter. For example, 'there are no company pension plans other than those set forth in the disclosure letter'.

Qualifications

[413] Frequently, the party providing a representation will qualify the representation by knowledge or materiality. For example, a representation regarding environmental liabilities may state that 'to the knowledge of the company' there are no environmental liabilities other than those set forth in the disclosure letter. This knowledge qualification can be the subject of significant negotiation. In an asset sale, the knowledge of the company is frequently defined as being the knowledge of certain senior officers of the company after having made inquiries. In a share transaction, the question of knowledge may be hotly debated since not all shareholders may have been involved in the running of the company and may not wish to provide a representation or may need to rely on other shareholders with respect to that representation.

[414] Another qualification that a vendor will negotiate is 'materiality'. A warranty may provide that there has been no material breach of a particular contract. Another formulation of the warranty may provide that there have been no breaches of environmental regulations, except for breaches that are not, in the aggregate, material. What constitutes 'materiality' is often difficult to negotiate. The vendor will typically want a dollar amount, whereas the purchaser will want to employ a more open-ended definition, such as 'material to the business taken as a whole'.

Standard Representations and Warranties

[415] Standard representations and warranties include:

- The vendor and purchaser corporate information is as represented and the entities are properly incorporated and continue to exist.
- The execution, delivery and performance of the agreement have been duly authorized and constitute a legal, valid and binding obligation.
- Books and records of the target corporation are complete and accurate, and financial statements have been presented in accordance with generally accepted accounting principles (GAAP).
- The target corporation has the corporate power to own its property and to carry on the business and has any licences required to carry on that business.
- The target corporation is not in violation of any agreements or applicable laws. Increasingly, there are also particular representations and warranties for compliance with privacy and anti-spam laws.
- The vendor satisfies residency requirements for income tax purposes or alternatively, a clearance certificate will be obtained to avoid withholding obligations under Canadian income tax legislation.
- The target corporation has title to the assets to be purchased (including with respect to intellectual property) or the vendors have title (unencumbered) to the shares being acquired.
- No person other than the purchaser has any option or right of first refusal (ROFR) or other similar right or privilege to acquire the assets or shares.
- All accounts receivable are bona fide and any doubtful debt deductions have been made in accordance with GAAP.
- Inventories are merchantable, fit for use, and sufficient to carry on the business in the ordinary course.
- Material contracts relating to the target corporation have been disclosed and these are not in default and, in an asset sale, may be assigned without the consent of the counterparty.

- The target corporation is not in breach of any real property leases or licences with respect to intellectual property.
- There are no undisclosed changes of control provisions in material contracts.
- There are no undisclosed environmental, pension or employee liabilities.

The foregoing is a list of merely some of the common representations and warranties. The representations and warranties will be tailored to the type of business and in the case of a share transaction may be extensive, covering every aspect of the business.

Survival

[416] Another area for negotiation will be the survival period for the representations and warranties following closing. Unless the representations and warranties are expressly stated to survive closing, they will merge with the closing and not continue. There is a wide variation in the survival period depending on the nature of the business and the respective bargaining power of the vendor and purchaser. In addition, the parties may have different survival periods for different types of representations. A survival period between six months and two years is not uncommon. However, certain representations and warranties should have a lengthy period of survival. For example, representations regarding tax matters should survive for as long as income tax authorities can reassess a prior tax filing and for the period of any appeals from those potential assessments.

Representations and Warranties Insurance

[417] In recent years, there has been a significant trend to use representations and warranties insurance (RWI) in private M&A transactions. RWI is a risk allocation product used in M&A transactions to primarily protect the insured party from losses and liabilities incurred as a result of breaches of representations and warranties set out in a purchase agreement. Through RWI, the insured can recover directly from the insurer for losses rather than from a party in the transaction.

[418] There are multiple benefits to purchasing RWI for a transaction. For sellers, RWI provides a way to reduce or eliminate the need for a traditional indemnity for breaches of representations and warranties and the risk of contingent liabilities. It can also reduce the need for holdbacks resulting in more proceeds being received at the closing of the transaction. For buyers, RWI is particularly helpful when the buyer is unable to obtain the desired level or duration of indemnification from the seller. Also, in an auction process, the bidder can use RWI to strategically distinguish its bid over others by lowering the customary level of indemnification. Although, conversely, there is a trend in auction processes whereby the sellers are requiring bidders to agree to have RWI in place as part of their bid submission. Further, RWI can be beneficial to the overall expediency of the transaction as it typically simplifies negotiations over the scope of the representations and warranties in the agreement. It is important to keep in mind that as an RWI policy can be obtained for either the buyer or the seller, seller-side policies will differ structurally from buyer-side policies to reflect the varying motivations of the insured party.

[419] Coverage of each RWI policy is bespoke to the transaction but is intended to cover the typical representations and warranties that would be given by a seller in an M&A transaction. The policy also covers liabilities for pre-closing taxes as a separate indemnity. However, RWI is not without limitations. Policies typically cover up to a certain amount for losses (most commonly, 10% of the purchase price). Therefore, the buyer may be at risk for extraordinary losses. Policies also typically do not cover: covenant breaches by the seller, purchase price adjustments, and losses resulting from breach of representations and warranties known by the buyer. As such, RWI should not be viewed as a replacement for due diligence by either party. Care and attention must be taken in drafting the RWI policies to ensure that essential policy terms, including the coverage amount, policy period, premium, retention, loss definition and exclusions, are clearly considered.

2.9.5 Pre-closing Covenants

[420] Prior to closing, the parties, particularly the vendor, will covenant to do certain things to facilitate the transfer of the business. These will include obtaining consent and regulatory approvals as well as continuing to conduct the business in a manner that is acceptable to the purchaser.

[421] The vendor will usually agree to obtain any consents required with respect to material contracts under assignment or change-of-control provisions. The parties will negotiate the level of effort required. The purchaser will want a 'best efforts' requirement, whereas the vendor may seek to shift some risk to the purchaser. In the common law provinces of Canada, most contracts may be assigned without the consent of the contracting party unless the agreement specifically requires consent. Similarly, unless a contract with a corporation has a change-of-control provision in it, the sale of the shares of that corporation ordinarily does not require any consent by the counterparty to the contract.

[422] A type of contract that cannot be assigned is an employment contract. Therefore, in an asset transaction, one of the pre-closing covenants will be for the purchaser to offer employment to the employees.

[423] As mentioned, another important pre-closing covenant will relate to the operation of the business. The vendor will agree to operate the business in the ordinary course until closing. In a share transaction, the target company will agree not to issue shares or options to acquire shares. The target company will also agree not to engage in a fundamental change or transactions outside of the ordinary course. In asset and share transactions, the parties will agree that transactions involving commitments or expenditures greater than a specified threshold amount will require the consent of the purchaser.

[424] Another pre-closing covenant may relate to regulatory clearances. For example, the parties may covenant to cooperate in obtaining clearances under such statutes as the *Competition Act*, the *Investment Canada Act* and the *Bank Act*.

2.9.6 Closing Conditions

[425] Considerable care will be taken in the drafting of closing conditions. From the purchaser's perspective, these conditions will be the basis on which the purchaser can walk away from the transaction. From the vendor's perspective, these conditions add deal risk. Closing conditions will usually provide that the condition may be waived by the party for whose benefit they have been inserted. If the conditions are not met and not waived, the agreement will typically provide for a cure period failing which the agreement may be terminated. The consequences, such as the necessity to pay a 'termination payment', will depend on the nature of the condition and which party failed to meet the condition. These consequences will be set out in the termination provisions of the agreement.

Typical closing conditions include the following:

- Representations and warranties of the vendor are usually 'brought down' to closing – that is, the vendor will deliver a certificate stating that the representations and warranties continue to be true as of the closing date.
- All necessary consents have been obtained with respect to assignments and all regulatory approvals have been obtained.
- The purchaser is satisfied with the results of any continuing due diligence.
- The vendor has complied with the covenant to operate the business in the ordinary course.
- There is no litigation seeking to prevent the closing of the transaction and no law, regulation or judicial or administrative order that would prevent the closing or make the closing illegal.
- All required documentation relating to title to assets has been delivered.
- There has been no material adverse change to the business or no fact, circumstance, event or change of law that would have a material adverse effect on the business.

All of these conditions may be qualified in some way. For example, the requirement that all representations and warranties continue to be true may be qualified for materiality.

2.9.7 Post-closing Covenants

[426] There are typically very few post-closing covenants except in the event of earn-out provisions. Some types of post-closing covenants are maintenance of books and records and, in asset transactions, possibly covenants to collect accounts receivable (assuming they were not part of the purchased assets), and the provision of transitional services. In share deals, there may be covenants with respect to the preparation and review of tax returns and the consequences of tax assessments.

2.9.8 Shareholder Approvals

Asset Sales

[427] An asset sale by the target corporation will require shareholder approval if it is a sale of all or substantially all of the assets of the target corporation. The resolution of the shareholders approving the sale must be passed by the affirmative vote of at least $66^{2}/_{3}\%$ of the shareholders present in person or by proxy at the meeting called for that purpose, subject to any unanimous shareholder agreement requiring a higher threshold for approval. Quite often the assets of a business are held in an operating subsidiary. In some provinces, it is clear that the shareholders of the parent holding company are entitled to vote on the sale. In other statutes, it is not clear. However, it is generally prudent to permit those shareholders to vote unless the circumstances demonstrate that the shareholders would not have a reasonable expectation that they would be permitted to vote on a fundamental change to the corporate group. Shareholders may exercise dissent rights if the resolution is approved.

[428] The question of whether a sale, lease or exchange involves all or substantially all of the assets of a corporation involves a quantitative test and a qualitative test. There is no bright line to guide the directors. However, typically the disposition, lease or exchange of more than 70% of the assets of the corporation by value is considered to be a sale of substantially all of the corporation or at least of a quantity that requires legal advice if no shareholder approval will be sought. The qualitative test involves analysing whether the sale, lease or exchange of assets would fundamentally change the nature of the corporation or its business. If it would, then the sale requires the approval of the shareholders. If the sale involves all or substantially all of the assets of the corporation, shareholder approval will be required.

Share Purchase

[429] Conceptually, a share purchase is a consensual process. However, Canadian private companies frequently have shareholder agreements in place with 'shotgun' provisions, rights of first refusal or offer, and 'drag-along' or 'tag-along' rights.

[430] A shotgun provision is a situation in which the triggering shareholder can force other shareholders to either sell their shares to the triggering shareholder at a price or buy that triggering shareholder's shares. These provisions must be followed scrupulously if they are to be triggered.

[431] A ROFR may require a selling shareholder receiving an offer from a bona fide arm's-length third party to first offer to sell the subject shares to the other existing shareholders. If the ROFR is not exercised by the other shareholders then the selling shareholder is free to sell to a third party on terms that are no more favourable than those that had been offered to the other shareholders. As with shotgun provisions, courts require shareholders to observe the provisions of ROFRs and will not allow shareholders to avoid their obligations through creative transactions. A right of first offer (ROFO) operates similarly to a ROFR but does not require the selling shareholder to have received an offer from a third party. Instead, the ROFO is triggered whenever the selling shareholder wants to exit. The shareholder must first offer the shares to other shareholders before the shareholder is permitted to market the shares to other parties.

[432] A shareholder agreement may also contain 'drag-along' or 'tag-along' rights. A drag-along right permits a selling shareholder (or a specified majority of shareholders) to require the other shareholders to sell their shares to a third party to whom the majority wishes to sell. A 'tag-along' right is similar only if it focuses on the right of the minority to participate in the sale on the same terms and conditions.

Amalgamation

[433] A statutory amalgamation will require shareholder approval. The resolution of the shareholders approving the amalgamation must be passed by the affirmative vote of at least 66$^{2}/_{3}$% of the shareholders present in person or by proxy at the meeting called for that purpose subject to any unanimous shareholder agreement requiring a higher threshold for approval. In some jurisdictions, the requisite shareholder approval is 75%. A statutory amalgamation requires approval by shareholders. Generally, all shareholders are entitled to vote (even classes of shares that would not ordinarily have voting rights). Shareholders may exercise dissent rights if the resolution is approved.

2.10 Role of the Courts

2.10.1 Organization

[434] Canadian courts are independent from other branches of government. All government action involving the exercise of a statutory power of decision is potentially subject to judicial review. Typically, all proceedings are open to the public unless there are overriding reasons of national security, protection of minors, or other compelling reasons for the court to order a closed hearing. Domestic and foreign litigants can expect to receive equal treatment by Canadian courts.

[435] Provincial Superior Courts have jurisdiction over all matters unless a statute has reserved the issue to a particular court. Provincial offences may be heard in a provincial court that is a lower court to the Superior Court. In addition, the Federal Court of Canada has jurisdiction over matters related to immigration, appeals from the Tax Court of Canada regarding federal taxation matters, and the enforcement of intellectual property rights, amongst other matters subject to federal legislation. The Federal Court also has concurrent jurisdiction with the provincial Superior Courts over competition law matters.

2.10.2 Jurisdiction over Foreign Persons

[436] Some provinces, such as British Columbia, have statutory provisions regarding jurisdiction. In other provinces, the general test for whether a Canadian court

[397] There are limited exceptions to the express consent requirement, in which case implied consent is sufficient. Many of these exceptions are time-limited. For example, an organization can send CEMs to individuals with whom it has an 'existing business relationship' for prescribed periods of time. The following are some additional examples of where implied consent is a permissible basis for sending CEMs:

- An organization may send a CEM to a recipient who has purchased or leased a product, goods, service, or land no more than two years immediately before the message was sent.
- An organization may send a CEM to a recipient who has accepted a business or investment opportunity no more than two years immediately before the message was sent.
- An organization may send a CEM to a recipient with whom it is in a written contract that is currently in existence or that expired less than two years immediately before the message was sent.
- An organization may send a CEM to a person who has been referred by someone with whom the organization is in an existing business relationship (and some other classes of relationship) provided the name of the referring party is disclosed in the message and the message states that it is being sent because of the referral.

[398] Moreover, some transaction-oriented communications are exempt from the consent requirements altogether, provided that the ***sole*** purpose of the communication falls within one of the following categories:

- provide a quote or estimate for the supply of a product, goods, a service, land or interest in land, if the quote or estimate was requested by the recipient;
- facilitate, complete or confirm a commercial transaction that the recipient previously agreed to enter into;
- provide warranty information, product recall information or safety or security information about a product, goods or service that the recipient has used or purchased;
- provide notification of factual information about an ongoing purchase, subscription, membership, account or loan of the recipient;
- provide employment or benefit plan information relating to employment or a plan in which the recipient is active;
- deliver a product, good or service, including product updates or upgrades that the recipient is entitled to receive under the terms of a transaction they have previously entered into.

CASL also prohibits the installation (or causing the installation) of a 'computer program' in the course of a commercial activity on another person's computer unless the recipient consents or a consent exception applies. These provisions apply if the computer system is located in Canada or the person installing or causing the installation is located in Canada.

has jurisdiction to hear and decide a civil claim is whether there is a 'real and substantial connection' between the court and either the subject matter or the defendant. A variety of factors have been considered by courts in determining whether or not there exists a requisite real and substantial connection in a particular matter. These include: whether the defendant is a resident of the jurisdiction, carries on business there, or markets its products or services there; whether the defendant has assets in the jurisdiction; whether a contract was entered into by the parties in the jurisdiction; and where the cause of action arose. In addition, a court has jurisdiction where the subject matter of the proceeding is real or personal property located in the jurisdiction.

[437] Even where a court determines that it does have jurisdiction to hear and determine a matter, under the doctrine of *forum non conveniens*, the court in a particular case may still decline to hear the matter if there is clearly a more appropriate jurisdiction than the domestic forum chosen by the plaintiff in which the case should be tried.

[438] The factors generally considered by Canadian courts in determining whether to exercise their discretion to decline to hear a matter include: (a) the relative convenience and expense for the parties to the proceeding and for their witnesses in litigating in the domestic court, as compared to any alternative forum; (b) the law to be applied to issues in the proceeding; (c) the desirability of avoiding multiplicity of legal proceedings; (d) the desirability of avoiding conflicting decisions in different courts; (e) the enforcement of an eventual judgment; (f) the fair and efficient working of the Canadian legal system as a whole; and (g) loss of any juridical advantage.

2.10.3 Conduct of Litigation

[439] The procedures followed in litigation vary considerably across Canada and by type of proceeding. The following is a discussion of some of the general procedural steps that are commonly part of most types of civil litigation.

[440] For most types of civil proceedings, the claim will initiate with 'pleadings' that contain the statement of allegations against the defendant or respondent. Parties will have the right to obtain documents relevant to the issues in the litigation from the other party. In most provinces, there is a positive onus on each party to produce relevant documents that are not subject to a privilege. The parties are then typically entitled to examine one representative of a corporation or witnesses.

[441] Prior to trial, there may be a mandatory mediation to settle the case. Only a small percentage of civil disputes are tried. Trials before juries in commercial disputes are uncommon. All Canadian provinces and the Federal Court now permit class proceedings.

[442] Costs are awarded against the losing party. However, there are rules that may increase or decrease the total cost award depending on prior offers to settle.

2.10.4 Arbitration

[443] It is not uncommon for commercial disputes to be arbitrated in Canada. Arbitration is voluntary and facilitated by arbitration legislation. Courts will generally enforce arbitration agreements if the parties have included one in their transaction agreement.

3 MERGER CONTROLS: ANTITRUST/ COMPETITION ISSUES

3.1 Relevant Legislation and Competent Authorities

3.1.1 Competition Bureau

[444] The Bureau administers and enforces the Competition Act (the 'Act'). Parties to certain types of transactions that exceed prescribed financial thresholds must notify the Commissioner of the transaction prior to closing. The Bureau determines whether to challenge a transaction on the basis of whether it will result, or is likely to result, in a substantial lessening or prevention of competition in a relevant market. If a transaction does not require notification, it may still be challenged within a three-year period following substantial completion of the transaction (or a one-year period if the parties make a voluntary filing). These rules apply equally to transactions undertaken by public and private companies.

Recent Amendments to the *Competition Act*

Parliament has amended the *Act* three times since 2022, with significant implications for M&A activity in Canada. These changes include:

- Repeal of the efficiencies defence, which previously could be used to secure clearance of a transaction that resulted in a substantial lessening or prevention of competition ('SLPC').
- Introduction of structural presumptions, pursuant to which a transaction that results in, or is likely to result in, certain increases in concentration and/or market share is presumed to result in an SLPC (the anti-competitive criteria for a remedy) unless the merging parties can prove otherwise on a balance of probabilities.
- Introduction of a higher standard for remedies to restore competition. The Tribunal, which decides contested mergers, is now empowered to issue remedial orders to 'restore' or 'preserve' competition to levels that would have prevailed but for the merger. Previously, jurisprudence required that only the substantial component of the SPLC effects be eliminated by a remedy.
- Extension of the limitation period for transactions not notified to the Bureau. The Bureau can now challenge transactions that are not subject to pre-merger notification for up to three years post-closing. The limitation period for challenging notified transactions (whether voluntary or mandatory) remains one year.

- Introduction of an automatic interim prohibition on closing where the Bureau seeks an injunction. There is now an immediate and automatic interim prohibition on closing a merger applicable from the point when the Bureau applies for an interim order to prevent closing until that application is heard and decided by the Tribunal.
- Broadening the scope of revenues included in notifiability calculations. In determining the relevant monetary thresholds for pre-merger notification, the Act now requires revenues from sales 'into' Canada (i.e., imports to Canada), in addition to sales 'in' and 'from' Canada, to be considered when determining whether the size-of-transaction threshold (currently CAD93 million) is exceeded. Mergers that were previously below the notification threshold because the threshold did not include revenues from imports to Canada may now trip this threshold.

3.1.2 Scope of the Controls

Notification

[445] There are two notification thresholds – the size of parties test and the size-of-transaction test. Both thresholds must be exceeded in order to trigger a notification requirement.

[446] The size of parties test is met if the parties to the transaction, together with their affiliates, have assets in Canada with an aggregate value of more than CAD400 million or annual gross revenues from sales in, from, or into Canada of more than CAD400 million.

[447] In an asset acquisition, the size-of-transaction threshold is met if the aggregate value of the assets in Canada, or the annual gross revenues from sales in, from or into Canada generated from all acquired assets (whether in Canada or otherwise), exceeds CAD93 million. This amount is reviewed and/or adjusted annually. The size-of-transaction test is different for a share acquisition. The test is met if the aggregate value of the assets in Canada of the corporation being acquired, or the annual gross revenues from sales in, from or into Canada exceeds CAD93 million, and the person or persons acquiring the shares, together with their affiliates, would own more than 20% of the voting shares in the case of a public corporation, or 35% in the case of a private corporation. If the acquiring party, together with its affiliates, already owns more than 20% of the voting shares of a public corporation, or more than 35% of a private corporation, notification would only be required if the proposed acquisition would result in the acquiring party, together with its affiliates, owning more than 50% of the voting shares of the corporation.

There are other tests for different transaction structures, such as amalgamations and other business combinations.

Exemptions from Pre-merger notification

[448] Certain types of transactions may be exempt from notification requirements. Examples include (but are not limited to): transactions among affiliates; certain types of joint ventures; acquisitions of real property or goods in the ordinary course of business (where the acquiror does not acquire substantially all of the assets of a business or an operating segment thereof); acquisitions of collateral or receivables; or an acquisition resulting from a foreclosure or default, or forming part of a debt workout made by a creditor; and acquisitions of certain Canadian resource properties where the buyer acquiring the property incurs expenses to carry out exploration or development activities.

Challenges to Mergers

[449] Any merger can be challenged by the Commissioner on the basis that it prevents or lessens, or is likely to prevent or lessen, competition substantially in any market (the SLPC standard), including with respect to labour markets.[1]

[450] If a merger is successfully challenged, the Tribunal may make a number of orders including prohibiting a proposed merger, requiring full or partial divestiture of assets for a completed merger, or dissolution of a completed merger. Under the recent amendments, merger remedies are to 'restore' or 'preserve' competition to levels that would have prevailed but for the merger – rather than the previous standard of addressing only the 'substantial' component of anti-competitive effects.

[451] If a transaction results in certain increases in concentration and/or market share, there is a rebuttable presumption of an SPLC required for a remedy. This 'significant increase in concentration or market share' is exceeded in circumstances where the transaction increases the concentration index by 100, and the total concentration index exceeds 1 800 or the combined market share of the parties exceeds 30%. The Herfindahl-Hirschman Index ('HHI') relied upon in the USA[2] will be used to determine industry concentration index in Canada. This new feature of the Act places the burden of proof to disprove anti-competitive effects on the merging parties where the relevant concentration thresholds are met, rather than the Bureau proving the opposite. Previously the Act specified that a merger could not be blocked based only on market share or concentration alone. These structural presumptions do not apply to any mergers that were notified or substantially completed before 20 June 2024.

[452] The Bureau has identified mergers that may substantially lessen competition as those that would enable the merged firm, whether unilaterally or in coordination with other entities, to sustain materially higher prices by diminishing existing competition. The Bureau historically considered the following types of mergers as being ones that could result in a SLPC:

- the acquisition of a potential entrant or of a recent entrant that was likely to expand or become a more vigorous competitor;

[1] A merger includes the acquisition or establishment, direct or indirect, by one or more persons, whether by purchase or lease of shares or assets, by amalgamation or by combination or otherwise, of control over or significant interest in the whole or a part of a business of a competitor, supplier, customer or other person.

[2] The HHI is defined as the sum of the squares of the market shares of all competitors in a market. The sum is small when there are many small firms and grows larger as the market becomes more concentrated, reaching 10 000 in a monopoly scenario.

- an acquisition by the market leader that pre-empts a likely acquisition of the same target by a competitor;
- the acquisition of an existing business that would likely have entered the market in the absence of the merger;
- an acquisition that prevents expansion into new geographic markets;
- an acquisition that prevents the pro-competitive effects associated with new capacity; and
- an acquisition that prevents or limits the introduction of new products.

[453] Third-party stakeholders have no standing to challenge a merger in the Tribunal. In that regard, the Commissioner's jurisdiction is exclusive. However, these stakeholders can complain to the Bureau, which complaints may, in turn, inform the Commissioner's position.

3.1.3 Process/Mechanics

Procedural Aspects

[454] Notifications are required from all parties to a notifiable transaction. The information required in the notifications will include, at a minimum, detailed information about the parties, the business and product lines of the company, principal suppliers and customers, future business plans and the reports or analyses prepared or received by senior officers for the purpose of analysing the proposed transaction. The parties must pay a CAD86 358.76 (as of 2024) filing fee. Once complete notifications are filed, the parties are not permitted to close until a thirty-day waiting period has expired. The Commissioner can issue a supplemental information request (SIR) within those thirty days. The information requirements of a SIR can be significant and compliance may take time. The parties may not complete the transaction until thirty days have expired from either the original filing of all information (if no SIR is issued) or until thirty days have expired from compliance with the requirements of a SIR.

[455] It is possible for the Bureau's review to take longer than the statutory waiting period. The parties may consummate the transaction (absent the Commissioner seeking an injunction); however, parties face a risk that the Commissioner could still challenge the transaction or seek remedies after the transaction has been completed. The waiting period does not affect the Commissioner's ability to seek a remedy, but the one-year (for notified transactions) and three-year (for non-notified transactions) limitation period, which run from closing, do operate to extinguish the Commissioner's ability to seek remedies.

Advance Ruling Certificate and No Action Letter

[456] Parties may also apply for an advance ruling certificate (an 'ARC') from the Bureau, which would generally preclude a later challenge to the transaction. The issuance of an ARC exempts parties from making a pre-merger notification; however, companies may choose to file both notifications and an ARC request. The parties may also seek a 'no action' letter and a statutory waiver of the obligation to notify and supply the prescribed filing information. A 'no action' letter does not preclude the Commissioner from later challenging the transaction but it will provide the parties with an indication that the Commissioner does not intend (based on the review) to seek an order from the Tribunal. The transaction could still be challenged for a period of up to one year from closing.

[457] Although it is possible for parties to engage with the Bureau while preparing a notification or applying for an advanced ruling certificate, it is recommended that they retain the assistance of specialized legal counsel with expert knowledge of the technical process.

3.1.4 Parallel Minister of Transport Review of Transactions Involving Federal Transportation Undertakings

[458] The Canada Transportation Act also requires a parallel review by the federal Minister of Transport of a proposed transaction notifiable to the Commissioner where such a transaction involves a 'federal transportation undertaking' (an undefined term that would likely encompass, for example, federally regulated air, rail, marine and truck transportation undertakings). A review under the *Canada Transportation Act* requires the Minister of Transport to assess whether the transaction raises any public interest issues in relation to national transportation, such as those in relation to economic, environmental, safety, security or social factors.

[459] Parties to transactions involving such federal transportation undertakings must, at the same time as they file the materials described above with the Commissioner, submit a notice to the Minister of Transport containing both (a) the information filed with the Commissioner and (b) a 'Public Interest Impact Assessment' addressing the potential transportation-related public interest impacts of the transaction. In addition to such analysis, the *Canada Transportation Act* notice must, among other things, contain a description of the relevant transportation undertaking(s) involved in the transaction; any proposed changes to the business or strategic plans relating thereto; proposed mitigation or remediation plans; as well as identification of major stakeholders and any consultation carried out. No filing fees are charged for a *Canada Transportation Act* notice.

[460] Where the Minister of Transport determines that no public interest issues are raised with the transaction, he or she is required to notify parties of that determination within 42 days of receiving the required notice. If, however, the Minister of Transport determines that such issues are raised, he or she may direct the Canadian Transportation Agency or any person to examine and report on those issues within 150 days. Where an examination is directed, the Commissioner must also produce a report to the Minister of Transport addressing any competition concerns in relation to the transaction. The parties are then afforded an opportunity to propose measures to address the concerns of the Minister of Transport and Commissioner, following which the former is required to make a recommendation to the Governor in Council as to whether it is in the public interest to approve the transaction. Under this more lengthy review process, the Governor in Council has the final authority to approve the transaction, with or without terms and conditions, or reject it.

3.2 Anti-competitive Restraints

[461] The purchaser of a business will typically want to ensure that the vendor does not start up or acquire a competing business. There are two mechanisms to prevent the re-entry of the vendor. One is to obtain a covenant that the vendor will not compete in the same or similar business. Another is to obtain a covenant that the vendor will not solicit former customers to another business. The non-competition covenant is, therefore, the broader of the two types of covenants. Not infrequently, these non-competition/non-solicitation covenants will be included in separate stand-alone agreements, or in employment agreements in the case of vendors who will continue as employees of the purchaser.

[462] Non-competition and non-solicitation agreements are restraints on trade and are enforced by the parties through litigation. Courts will enforce these covenants if they are reasonable in relation to the nature and value of the goodwill being acquired by the purchaser.

[463] There are no individual or block exemptions for anti-competitive restraints. Rather, in determining whether the restriction is reasonable, the court will have regard to the following considerations:

- The subject matter of the covenant. A non-competition covenant that is narrowly focused on the actual business of the vendor or a non-solicitation covenant that is focused on the clients of the vendor is more likely to be enforced than one that extends to associated businesses.
- The geographical scope of the restriction. The geographical area must be precisely described. The geographical area must be rationally related to the goodwill being protected. If neither the purchaser nor the vendor has operations in Europe, it is likely to be difficult to convince a court that it was necessary to restrict the vendor's activities in Europe in order to protect the goodwill of the business.
- The temporal duration of the restriction. The duration of the restriction must be rationally related to the investment in the goodwill of the business. The court will consider the size of the investment and the length of time that it would take (depending on the nature of the business) to secure the benefit of the goodwill from the vendor. Durations of greater than three years become more difficult to justify.
- Apart from the risk that overbroad covenants may not be enforceable, it is possible that in some cases, they may raise criminal risks under the *Act*'s conspiracy provisions.

[464] For a discussion on non-competition and non-solicitation agreements in the employment context, *see* the '*Retention of Key Personnel*' section below. Please note that courts are generally more likely to enforce a non-compete in the context of a sale of a business than in the employment context.

4 TAXATION ASPECTS

4.1 Nature of the Tax Regime

[465] Canada imposes taxes on Canadian resident corporations on their worldwide income and imposes taxes on non-resident corporations that carry on business in Canada or dispose of 'taxable Canadian property' (subject to certain limitations where an applicable income tax treaty or convention applies). Similarly, all of the provinces impose income taxes on such corporations. In addition, provinces impose a limited capital tax on certain corporations that are financial institutions. Realized capital gains net of capital losses ('net capital gains') are also subject to tax. In the recent past, half of net capital gains were included in a taxpayer's income. The 2024 Canadian Federal Budget ('Budget 2024') proposes to increase the inclusion rate for capital gains realized on or after 25 June 2024 from one-half to two-thirds for corporations and trusts.

[466] Canadian federal and provincial governments may use income tax legislation to create fiscal incentive regimes to encourage sectoral investment. For example, there may be special provisions for businesses operating in the oil and gas, mineral exploration or green energy sectors, for those operating in certain geographical regions in which the government wishes to encourage investment, or for certain scientific and experimental development.

[467] Canada has entered into numerous tax treaties that may reduce or eliminate double taxation resulting from a corporation being subject to tax in another country, as well as in Canada. These tax treaties essentially allocate the jurisdiction to tax between the two jurisdictions to prevent double taxation. For example, if a corporation is found to be resident in two countries pursuant to the domestic legislation of those countries, most tax treaties will deem residence to be in one jurisdiction. The Canada-United States Tax Convention (the 'Canada-US Tax Convention'), for example, provides that residency will be in the country in which the corporation was created or continued if those laws are of either Canada or the US. If the corporation is a US-resident corporation carrying on business in Canada, Canada may tax the non-resident corporation's Canadian source business profits to the extent those profits are attributable to a permanent establishment of the non-resident corporation in Canada. Determining what constitutes a 'permanent establishment' under the Canada-US Tax Convention is not always straightforward. However, it will generally include any office, branch or fixed place of business of a non-resident corporation in Canada and may also include situations where services are performed in Canada by the non-resident corporation or where an employee has and habitually exercises the authority to conclude contracts in the name of the non-resident corporation.

4.2 Liability to Tax

[468] To determine its taxable income a corporation may deduct expenses reasonably related to the earning of that income. In addition, certain amounts, including taxable dividends received from a taxable Canadian corporation and certain amounts received from foreign affiliates carrying on an active business as dividend income may generally be deducted. Since 2006, non-capital or business losses may be carried back three years and forward twenty years to reduce taxable income in those years. Generally, net capital losses may be carried back three years and forward indefinitely but may only be applied against taxable capital gains. It is important to note that an acquisition of control of a corporate taxpayer will extinguish the corporation's net capital loss carry-overs and any non-capital loss carry-overs will only be deductible against future income from the same or similar business in which the losses were incurred.

[469] There are a number of taxes and duties that are relevant to operating in Canada, which should be mentioned briefly:

- *Commodity and Sales Taxes*. Canada's commodity and sales tax regime is complex. The federal goods and services tax ('GST') is a value added tax imposed on most goods and services supplied in Canada. A corporation involved in making available taxable supplies in Canada in the course of a commercial activity may be required to register for and charge, collect and remit GST on these supplies. In addition, many provinces have harmonized their provincial sales tax with the GST. This includes Nova Scotia, New Brunswick, Prince Edward Island, Newfoundland and Labrador and Ontario. The rate of the harmonized sales tax ('HST') varies among these jurisdictions depending on the rate of the provincial component. Quebec has a separate provincial sales tax regime which closely resembles the GST and British Columbia, Saskatchewan and Manitoba have distinct provincial sales tax regimes.
- *Land Transfer Taxes*. Most provinces levy a tax on the acquisition of real property. In addition, Ontario's largest city, the City of Toronto, also levies a land transfer tax.
- *Customs Duties*. Customs duties may be levied on the importation of goods into Canada. Canada applies different duty rates (preferential and non-preferential) to the same goods on the basis of their origin. Moreover, certain products may be subject to anti-dumping duties. The amount of duties is calculated by reference to their classification and applicable duty rate set out under the List of Tariff Provisions in the Schedule to the Customs Tariff. The duty rate is calculated upon the value for duty, which is determined in accordance with the *Customs Act*.
- *Excise Duties*. Spirits, beer, tobacco, cannabis and related products are subject to a special tax called excise duties.

4.2.1 Canadian Branch Operations

[470] Non-resident corporations who carry on business in Canada, directly, rather than through a Canadian subsidiary, are subject to a tax in respect of the after-tax branch profits of the corporation that are remitted outside of Canada. This tax is commonly referred to as a 'branch tax' and is a rough equivalent to the withholding tax which would otherwise be payable on any dividends paid by a Canadian subsidiary to its foreign parent corporation.

[471] This 'branch tax' is payable at the rate of 25% of the after-tax profits of the branch operations not being reinvested in Canada. This rate may be reduced under certain tax treaties to 10% or 15%. Under the Canada-US Tax Convention, the rate has been further reduced in certain circumstances to 5%. Furthermore, a tax treaty between Canada and a foreign jurisdiction may exempt the first CAD500 000 of income that may otherwise be subject to branch tax.

4.2.2 Canadian Subsidiary Corporations

[472] A foreign entity is not generally subject to Canadian income tax merely by carrying on business in Canada through a Canadian subsidiary. The Canadian subsidiary will, however, be subject to Canadian taxes as a Canadian resident. This will include income tax on the Canadian subsidiary's worldwide income unless an income tax treaty or convention determines otherwise.

[473] Dividends distributed to the non-resident parent corporation will be subject to withholding taxes at a rate of 25%. However, the withholding tax rate is reduced to 10% or 15% under most of Canada's tax treaties. In addition, the Canada–US Tax Convention, and certain other treaties, provides that the rate will be further reduced in certain circumstances to 5%.

4.2.3 Taxation of Dividends

[474] Residents of Canada receiving eligible taxable dividends (frequently, those received from a larger corporation) must gross-up those dividends for tax purposes but will also be entitled to a dividend tax credit. As of 2024, the gross-up is 38% and the federal dividend tax credit is calculated as six-eleventh of the gross-up (or 15.0198% of the grossed-up dividends). Dividends other than eligible taxable dividends are grossed-up by 15%. The federal dividend tax credit is calculated as nine-thirteenth of the gross-up (or 9.0301% of the grossed-up dividends).

4.3 Tax Considerations Arising on M&A Transactions

4.3.1 Asset Purchase Versus Share Purchase

[475] Non-tax considerations come into play when determining whether an M&A transaction will be structured as an asset or a share purchase. For example, the purchaser may wish to only acquire the business assets and not risk acquiring any (or certain) liabilities. This would not be possible in a share purchase (although liabilities can be covered with representations and indemnities). Tax considerations also arise when determining whether an M&A transaction should be structured as an asset transaction or a share transaction.

4.3.2 Asset Purchase

[476] Asset purchase structures tend to be more beneficial to the purchaser than to the vendor. From a tax perspective, the purchase price will be allocated among the acquired assets to determine the tax costs of those assets to the purchaser. The purchaser may be able to allocate the tax cost to assets that depreciate from a tax perspective more quickly so as to maximize the capital cost allowance for the assets starting in the year of purchase. To the extent the purchase price is in excess of the tax cost of the assets, the purchaser will benefit from an increase in the overall tax cost to the assets following the purchase. This could result in additional tax depreciation becoming available to the purchaser.

[477] However, asset sales may not be advantageous to the vendor. The asset sale may generate capital gains and business income for the target corporation. The capital cost allowance previously deducted by the target corporation may be recaptured in whole or in part depending on the allocation of the purchase price to that asset. The corporation will be subject to tax and the individual shareholders will also be subject to tax on dividends distributed to them. Non-resident vendors are subject to Canadian withholding taxes on dividends.

4.3.3 Share Purchase

[478] Share purchase transactions tend to be more beneficial to the vendor than to the purchaser. If the vendor is a Canadian resident, the sale of shares will generally produce a capital gain. Only 50% of the capital gain will be taxable for the Canadian resident vendors. Furthermore, the gain may be subject to a lifetime capital gains exemption of CAD1.25 m as proposed in Budget 2024, and yet to be enacted as of the date of the writing of this volume (to be indexed annually for inflation as of 2026) if shares of the target company are qualified small business corporation shares (QSBC shares). The following criteria must be met for a target share to be a QSBC share:

- at the time of sale, it was a share of the capital stock of a 'small business corporation' (*see* below), and it was owned by the vendor, the vendor's spouse or common law partner, a trust or a partnership of which the vendor was beneficiary or a member;
- throughout the 24 months immediately before the share was disposed of, while the share was owned by the vendor, a partnership of which the vendor was a member, a trust of which the vendor was a beneficiary or a person related to the vendor, it was a share of a Canadian-controlled private corporation and more than 50% of the fair market value of the assets of the corporation were:
  - used mainly in an active business carried on primarily in Canada by the Canadian-controlled private corporation, or by a related corporation;
  - certain shares or debts of connected corporations; or
  - a combination of these two types of assets;

- throughout the twenty-four months immediately before the share was disposed of, no one owned the share other than the vendor, a partnership of which the vendor was a member or a person related to the vendor.

Generally, a small business corporation is a Canadian-controlled private corporation and all or substantially all (generally understood to mean 90% or more) of the fair market value of its assets is attributable to assets used principally in an active business carried on primarily in Canada by the corporation or a related corporation (whether directly or indirectly, through equity or debt interests in another small business corporation).

[479] There may be different considerations for a non-resident shareholder of a target entity. Generally, capital gains realized by a non-resident shareholder that is not otherwise subject to tax in Canada could be exempt from Canadian income tax. An exception to this exemption arises if the property disposed of is 'taxable Canadian property'. In the case of a private company, the shares will only be taxable Canadian property if, at any time in the previous sixty months, they derived more than 50% of their value from real property situated in Canada, resource property situated in Canada, timber property situated in Canada or options or interests in any of the above. In such a case, a non-resident vendor may be subject to withholding taxes but ultimately may be exempt from Canadian tax on a share sale under the terms of an applicable income tax treaty.

[480] From the purchaser's perspective, the entire purchase price will be allocated to the cost of the shares. There is only a limited ability to increase the tax cost of certain types of property inside the corporation on an acquisition of control. Outside of these specific rules, there will be no adjustment to the tax cost of the assets. Furthermore, there may be some unfavourable tax consequences for the target corporation. In Canada, a corporation is deemed to have a fiscal year-end immediately before an acquisition of control. This accelerates the expiration of non-capital loss carry-forwards. Moreover, net capital losses, which arise from the disposition of assets at less than the adjusted cost base of those assets, are deemed to expire. Any accrued losses on inventory, accounts receivable, or non-depreciable property are also deemed to be realized. These rules are all designed to prevent purchasers from shopping for losses.

[481] There are however certain situations in which a share purchase transaction may be tax advantageous to a purchaser. If the target corporation has large non-capital losses from prior years, the purchaser may be able to structure its affairs to permit the use of those losses against future income. These losses may be applied for twenty years from the date of the loss against future income from the same or similar business as that which generated the loss, provided that the loss business is carried on with a reasonable expectation of profit.

4.3.4 Tax-Deferred Transfers and Tax-Deferred Amalgamations

[482] The *Income Tax Act* (Canada)(the 'Tax Act') permits a variety of tax-deferred transactions that may be beneficial to restructure a corporate group.

Section 85 Rollover

[483] Section 85 permits the transfer of property to a corporation on a tax-deferred basis in certain transactions where the corporation provides its own shares as consideration for the property. The seller and the purchasing corporation must jointly execute a prescribed election form and file it with the Canada Revenue Agency in the prescribed time. The elected amount cannot be less than the tax cost to the taxpayer of the property and it cannot be more than the fair market value of the property. In addition, the elected amount cannot be less than the fair market value of any non-share consideration received by the transferor. The seller may be a Canadian or non-Canadian. However, the purchaser must be a 'taxable Canadian corporation'. The seller must also receive at least one share of capital stock of the purchasing corporation. The seller may also receive non-share consideration, which may include cash, promissory notes, the assumption of debt or any other property. Real property or an interest in real property owned by a non-resident that is not used in a business carried on in Canada by such non-resident may not be subject to the rollover.

Section 85.1: Share-for-Share Exchanges

[484] Section 85.1 allows a vendor to transfer shares to another corporation for treasury shares of the purchasing corporation on a tax-deferred basis if:

- the purchaser is a Canadian corporation;
- the shares being sold by the seller are of a taxable Canadian corporation and are held as capital property;
- the purchaser corporation issues its own shares to the vendor as consideration; and
- the only consideration the vendor receives is shares of one particular class of the purchaser corporation.

In addition, the transaction will not qualify for treatment under section 85.1 if it has any of the following characteristics:

- the vendor and purchaser were, immediately before the exchange, not dealing with each other at arm's length;
- immediately after the exchange, the vendor or persons not dealing at arm's length with the vendor, alone or together, controlled the purchaser or beneficially owned more than 50% of the value of all outstanding shares of the purchaser;
- a section 85 election was filed in respect of the transaction to which the particular taxpayer is a party; or
- non-share consideration was received by the vendor for the transferred shares.

[485] If the conditions are met, the tax deferral automatically applies and no election need be filed. The tax cost of the transferred shares to the purchaser corporation is the lesser of the fair market value of the shares and the paid-up capital of the shares, immediately before the exchange.

[486] In order to realize these benefits, a typical exchangeable share transaction involving a foreign company would involve the incorporation of a Canadian subsidiary acquisition company that would acquire the shares of the target corporation and issue to the vendors its shares that are exchangeable into shares of the non-resident parent corporation.

Amalgamations

[487] A tax deferral can also be offered to shareholders of corporations where an amalgamation is carried out that satisfies the requirements of section 87 of the Tax Act.

[488] Section 87 contemplates horizontal, vertical and three-cornered, or triangular amalgamations. A three-cornered amalgamation arises where a target corporation amalgamates with the subsidiary of another corporation and consideration provided to the target shareholders is shares of the parent corporation (rather than the amalgamated corporation) These types of amalgamations can be especially helpful where the parent and the target are not formed under the laws of the same jurisdiction.

[489] Under the amalgamation structure, the amalgamated corporation is the successor of both amalgamating corporations. It succeeds, therefore, in all of the rights, liabilities and obligations of the predecessor companies.

4.4 Withholding Taxes

[490] Canada imposes withholding taxes on certain payments made by a Canadian resident to a non-resident on most forms of income from property including dividends, rents, royalties and certain interest payments. The base rate is 25% but may be reduced as a result of the application of a bilateral tax treaty or convention. With respect to withholding tax on interest payments, interest paid to a non-resident who is dealing at arm's length with the Canadian payor, and who is not participating in debt interest, is generally not subject to withholding tax.

[491] In addition, Canada imposes withholding taxes (15% federally and, in some cases, an additional provincial amount for Québec) on amounts paid to a non-resident for services rendered in Canada if those services are not in the course of regular and continuous employment.

[492] As mentioned above, if a non-resident disposes of property which is 'taxable Canadian property' withholding and reporting obligations arise under section 116 of the Tax Act. Pursuant to these rules, the non-resident is required to notify the Canada Revenue Agency and obtain a clearance certificate (by evidencing that no tax is payable or by pre-paying the tax). Even if there is no tax payable under a tax treaty or the sale results in a capital loss, notification will generally be required. In addition to penalties, the Tax Act imposes a joint liability on the purchaser for the non-resident vendor's tax liability if a clearance certificate is not obtained when required under the Tax Act.

4.5 Thin Capitalization

[493] Canada restricts the amount of interest a corporation resident in Canada may deduct on loans made by non-residents who are the Canadian resident corporation's significant shareholders or their affiliates. As a general rule, the ratio of the debt owing to the non-resident parent or other non-resident affiliate to the paid-up capital, surplus and retained earnings of the Canadian subsidiary should not exceed 1.5 to 1, or all interest payments will be disallowed.

4.6 Transfer Pricing

[494] Canada's transfer pricing regime conforms to the OECD arm's-length principle. Taxpayers who are parties to non-arm's length transactions with non-residents must contemporaneously document their transfer pricing transactions as well as the steps taken to establish that the terms and conditions of the transaction are what would have been expected if the parties were dealing at arm's length.

4.7 Excessive Interest and Financing Expenses Limitation

[495] Canada recently enacted new interest deductibility limitation rules. The Excessive Interest and Financing Expense Limitation (EIFEL) rules apply to taxation years that begin on or after 1 October 2023.

[496] These interest deductibility limits restrict the amount of net interest and financing expenses (IFEs) (being interest and financing expenses net of interest and financing revenues) that may be deducted by a taxpayer (or by a group) to 30% of 'adjusted taxable income' – which is calculated on a basis similar to earnings before interest, taxes, depreciation and amortization, also known as 'EBITDA'. The definition of 'taxpayer' in the EIFEL rules excludes natural persons and partnerships thereby limiting the scope of these deductibility limits to corporations and trusts. However, these deductibility limits apply to corporations or trusts that hold an interest in a partnership to the extent of their share of net interest and financing expenses from the partnership. IFEs that are denied under these rules can be carried forward indefinitely and deducted in a future taxation year where there is additional capacity. Generally, the EIFEL rules do not apply to a Canadian resident corporation in a taxation year if its total net IFEs are less than USD1 m in the particular year.

4.8 Hybrid Mismatch

[497] Canada recently enacted certain hybrid mismatch rules which apply retroactively to payments arising on or after 1 July 2022. These rules are intended to implement the recommendations in, and be generally consistent with, the report under Action 2 of the Group of 20 and Organisation for Economic Co-operation and Development's Base Erosion and Profit Shifting Project (the 'BEPS Action 2 Report'), titled Final Report on Neutralising the Effects of Hybrid Mismatch Arrangements. 'Hybrid mismatch arrangements' are cross-border arrangements that exploit differences in the income tax treatment of business entities or financial instruments under the laws of two or more countries to produce mismatches in tax results (referred to as 'hybrid mismatches').

[498] Consistent with the recommendations in the BEPS Action 2 Report, the Canadian hybrid mismatch rules eliminate hybrid mismatches and align the tax results in Canada and the other relevant countries in respect of a mismatch, by restricting the amount deductible by a taxpayer in respect of a payment under a hybrid mismatch arrangement, or including an amount in the income of a taxpayer who receives such a payment, as applicable. The new legislation addresses deduction/non-inclusion mismatches that arise from payments where the mismatch is attributable to the terms of a particular financial instrument.

5 EMPLOYMENT CONSIDERATIONS

[499] Minimum employment standards, including minimum compensation entitlements and working conditions, are set by provincial legislation or, in the case of FWUBs, by federal legislation. In the private sector, FWUBs include entities such as banks, airlines, and interprovincial railways, as well as all businesses operating in the territories unless there is specific territorial legislation that governs them.

[500] In addition to minimum employment standards legislation, unionized workplaces are also governed by applicable labour relations legislation. Labour relations legislation prescribes the formation of collective agreements and the process of resolving labour relations disputes involving trade unions. The legislation does not distinguish between the standards applicable to 'white collar' and 'blue collar' employees although trade workers are generally more likely to be unionized and subject to the legislation applicable to unions.

[501] Unless specifically contracted out of, the common law governs the formation of individual employment contracts in each of the provinces and territories outside of Québec. In Québec, the *Civil Code* governs the formation of employment contracts.

5.1 Minimum Standards

[502] Canadian employment law contains minimum standards with respect to wages, hours of work, overtime, holidays, vacation pay, parental leaves, and termination and severance pay. These minimum standards cannot be waived or contracted out of by employees. However, employers may offer more generous terms of service, also known as 'greater right or benefit'. Unilateral deductions from an employee's wages (without employee authorization) are generally not permitted except as required by law (such as deductions for federal and provincial income tax, Canada Pension Plan contributions or Employment Insurance Plan contributions) or benefit plan premiums if an employee is entitled to receive benefits, such as life insurance or supplementary medical benefits.

[503] In recent years, there have been a number of class actions in which employees and former employees have sought compensation for past, unpaid overtime pay entitlements. With specific exceptions for certain professions, types of employment and certain managers, Canadian employees are generally entitled to overtime pay. In an era in which employees may be connected to the office virtually over the Internet and expected to respond to electronic messages or issues that arise outside of normal business hours, overtime pay entitlements may be difficult to manage. Employers are permitted to allow employees to 'bank' overtime in most jurisdictions and take that time off in lieu of payment subject to applicable employment standards laws. Purchasers of businesses may wish to conduct due diligence regarding past and ongoing compliance with Canadian minimum compensation standards, including overtime, to determine any potential liability.

[504] In the context of mergers and acquisitions, the transfer of employment relationships is treated differently, depending on whether the transaction is an asset deal or a share deal. Within the context of a share deal, employment automatically transfers, whereas, in the context of an asset deal, employment does not automatically transfer. Regardless, it is best practice to enter into new employment agreements with employees, effective as of the close of the transaction. If the employees continue with the new employer, their past service with the former employer becomes an implied term in the new employment contract unless the contract expressly provides otherwise. This means that the employee retains all of the minimum legislated employment entitlements associated with their length of service, including vacation leave, notice of termination or pay in lieu of notice, and severance pay. This could become very important in the event of a subsequent termination from employment. Termination and change-of-control provisions in employment contracts with the former employer should also be noted, as these provisions may have an impact on a purchaser's liability. A purchaser must, therefore, fully investigate the nature of the vendor's labour and employment relations and liabilities in the context of the applicable successor rights laws.

[505] Employers do not have an obligation to inform or consult with their employees regarding a potential sale of the business. They are also generally not obligated to inform or consult with employees regarding mass redundancies or proposed layoffs and changes in pension schemes unless the employees are unionized. Employees are also not automatically entitled to management representation or directorship positions on the board. Work councils do not play a significant role in Canada.

5.2 Labour Relations/Trade Union Legislation

[506] Canadian federal and provincial labour laws permit employees to unionize by forming a bargaining unit, which employers are required to recognize (once certified by the applicable provincial or federal labour relations board). From that point, the union is the exclusive bargaining agent for the bargaining unit. Once a collective agreement is reached between the employer and the union, no strikes or lockouts are permitted during the term of the agreement. Disputes that may arise, including those relating to individual employees, must be resolved through a grievance process, which may involve going to private mediation, arbitration or conciliation and are not dealt with through the public court process.

[507] Canadian labour relations legislation imposes significant successor rights for unionized employees on the sale of a business. The purchaser of all or part of a business will typically be bound to the current collective agreements, even in an asset purchase transaction.

5.3 Pension and Benefits Plans

[508] Federal and provincial governments provide pension, benefit and welfare programmes. However, employers may also offer private pension plan benefits. These pension plans are registered with the provincial or federal government, based on jurisdiction, and must comply with income tax legislation to be afforded preferential tax treatment. Federal and provincial legislation governs pension plans.

[509] The two main types of employer-sponsored pension plans are either defined benefit or defined contribution plans. In recent years, there has been significant litigation relating to the duties of the administrators of these plans as well as to the conflicts of interest that may arise when the administrator of the plan is also the employer sponsor of the plan. Administrators of the plan have fiduciary obligations to the plan members. In cases of underfunded defined benefit plans, administrators have been sued by plan members who allege irresponsible or inadequate investment policies. Employers who both sponsor and administer the plan have been sued for conflicts of interest in preferring their own interests over those of the plan members.

5.4 Retention of Key Personnel

[510] Under Canadian law, an employee cannot be forced to continue working for a new employer following a merger or acquisition. Instead, the retention of key personnel is often achieved by negotiating favourable employment contracts with these employees to ensure that they will continue with the new employer and to dissuade them from joining competitors. Where key employees are indispensable to the success of the business they may be referenced in a schedule to the purchase agreement highlighting their significance to the transaction.

[511] It is also possible for the new employer to rely on restrictive covenants, such as non-compete or non-solicitation agreements, as a defensive tactic, to prevent key personnel from competing with the new employer or soliciting the new employer's clients and staff. During due diligence, it is important for an acquirer to consider the enforceability of any existing non-competition and non-solicitation provisions in the employment contracts of the target's employees. These provisions must be drafted reasonably and precisely. Any ambiguity will be interpreted in favour of the employee. For example, if a non-solicitation or non-competition provision refers to a geographic area, this area must have a precise boundary. The use of a phrase such as 'the greater Toronto area' may result in a court declining to enforce the provision since the boundaries of that area are not clearly defined. Restrictive covenants will not be 'read down' by the courts, and if one part of the provision is unenforceable, the whole provision is considered unenforceable.

[512] Generally, non-solicitation provisions that prohibit the employee from soliciting the customers and employees of the company after departure will be enforceable if it is for a reasonable duration and of a reasonable scope. It is unlikely that a covenant not to solicit any current or future customer (irrespective of whether the employee had a relationship with that customer) for an indefinite or lengthy period of time will be enforced by a court. By contrast, a non-solicitation provision that is limited to the customer accounts with which the employee dealt and for a period of two years or less could be enforced if there was a material risk that the confidential information of the company could be used to entice those customers to leave the organization.

[513] Non-competition provisions are very difficult to enforce, particularly if a non-solicitation clause can adequately protect the employer's interests. In Canada (with the exception of Ontario), a non-competition clause is prima facie unenforceable unless it is shown to be reasonable. In Ontario, non-competition clauses and agreements more generally are banned altogether, except in very narrow circumstances. A non-competition clause must be reasonable in relation to its scope (including geographical scope) and duration. Courts will generally not interfere with an employee's right to work in his or her chosen field. The court will be especially hostile to enforcing a non-competition provision with respect to employees who are not executives or senior managers with access to significant confidential business information. When dealing with lower-level employees, courts will generally expect organizations to rely on non-disclosure agreements. However, a non-competition agreement for a well-defined type of activity, in a small geographical area for a period of one or two years is much more likely to be enforceable than a broad non-competition agreement.

[514] As a result of the potential unenforceability of these provisions, it is common to include separate clauses in an employment contract dealing with non-disclosure, non-solicitation and non-competition. Assuming that the agreement has a severability clause, the failure of one of the provisions to be enforced may not be fatal to the other provisions.

[515] Acquirers should be wary of relying on non-competition or non-solicitation agreements entered into by existing employees. If entered into following the commencement of employment, these agreements require appropriate consideration. Examples of additional consideration could be a signing bonus, raise, or extended vacation benefits.

[516] Outside of Ontario, an exception to the general reluctance of courts to enforce non-competition provisions is where the employee is a fiduciary employee, particularly if the employee is a founder. In this case, a non-competition provision tied to the sale of the business is much more likely to be enforceable, although it will still need to meet the criterion of reasonableness. The court will consider whether the duration, scope of prohibited activities and geographical scope are reasonable in light of the goodwill being acquired by the purchaser. In Ontario, non-competition agreements are permitted if the employee is an 'executive', which includes CEOs, Presidents, or other chief executive positions.

5.5 Termination of Employment

[517] With very few exceptions for certain appointed positions or for fixed-term employment contracts, all employees are entitled to statutory notice or pay in lieu of termination of their employment without cause. In Canada, employment is not 'at will'. Upon termination without cause, employees are entitled to, at minimum, the notice prescribed in provincial or federal legislation. For example, in Ontario, employees are generally entitled to one week's notice (or pay in lieu of such notice) for each year of employment to a maximum of eight weeks. In order to limit an employee's termination pay to only the entitlements outlined in legislation, the employment contract must contain an enforceable termination clause. Otherwise, an employee may be entitled to common law reasonable notice. There is no exact formula for common law reasonable notice, but it is typically months of notice (or pay in lieu), as opposed to weeks. The length of notice under the common law will depend on the length of service, type of employment, age of the employee and other factors relevant to determining what would be reasonable in the employee's specific circumstances. In recent years, courts in Canada have awarded greater reasonable notice periods, particularly in the context of older employees who have worked for a significant amount of time for an employer.

[518] Employment standards legislation may also require payment of severance payments in some cases. For example, in Ontario, in cases where the dismissal is part of the permanent discontinuance of a business involving the termination of fifty or more employees within six months or less or an employer has an annual global payroll of CAD2.5 m or more, employees with five years' service or more are entitled to severance pay. Severance pay in Ontario is equal to approximately one week per year of employment to a maximum of twenty-six weeks.

5.6 Occupational Health and Safety

[519] Canadian occupational health and safety legislation exists federally and in every province in Canada. This legislation is intended to prevent workplace accidents, although, in some provinces, such as Ontario, the legislation extends to address workplace harassment, violence and sexual harassment. Employers are

obligated to take all reasonable precautions to protect the health and safety of employees. In some provinces, occupational health and safety laws apply to both employees and independent contractors working on the employer's premises. The legalization of cannabis in Canada has also brought with it a new set of workplace safety issues that employers must address.

[520] Occupational health and safety involves a combination of minimum standards and duties, which are enforced through occupational health and safety inspections, as well as employee participation in occupational health and safety committees. There are typically prescribed minimum duties and frequency of meetings for these committees, which discuss health and safety concerns in the workplace and make recommendations. In addition, employees have the right to be informed regarding hazards and may refuse to work in unsafe working conditions.

[521] It should also be noted that the *Criminal Code* imposes criminal liability for unsafe workplaces. While charges under the *Criminal Code* are not common, in particularly egregious accidents employers and/or supervisors may be charged.

5.7 Workers' Compensation

[522] Canadian workers' compensation legislation provides for no-fault insurance with respect to workplace illnesses and injuries. In certain designated industries or, in some provinces, if an employer has any employees in the province, participation is compulsory for Canadian employers and the benefits provided under the insurance plan are the employee's exclusive remedy for a workplace injury. Workers' compensation is governed at the provincial and territorial levels.

[523] Under workers' compensation legislation, employers register with the applicable governmental agency and make contributions to the insurance fund. Premiums are intended to reflect the relative risk of a workplace based on the type of industry. In addition, the workplace's claims history may affect premiums. In addition, employers are required to report workplace accidents and occupational illnesses within prescribed periods of time, engage in injury prevention activities, and assist employees in returning to work (possibly with modified duties).

5.8 Human Rights Legislation

[524] Canadian federal and provincial human rights legislation prohibits discrimination and provides for a system to investigate and resolve complaints with respect to allegations of discrimination. Although this legislation applies to a broad array of activities, there are provisions that specifically apply to employment, including recruiting. The prohibited grounds of discrimination vary among jurisdictions. In Ontario, every person has a right to equal treatment with respect to employment without discrimination because of race, ancestry, place of origin, colour, ethnic origin, citizenship, creed, sex (including pregnancy and breastfeeding), sexual orientation, gender identity, gender expression, age, record of offences, marital status, family status or disability. In addition, human rights legislation commonly contains provisions specifically dealing with harassment, including sexual harassment.

[525] Employers are prohibited from making employment decisions based on prohibited grounds of discrimination, including hiring, promotion, compensation and dismissal decisions. Discrimination need not be direct to violate human rights legislation. Human rights tribunals recognize that employment practices may indirectly affect persons as a result of a personal characteristic that is protected by human rights legislation, which also amounts to discrimination. These may include an occupational requirement that, for example, results in the disqualification of individuals based on physical disability. For example, the Ontario Human Rights Tribunal found that terminating an employee's health and life benefits at age 65 constitutes discrimination on the basis of age. Employers should keep this decision in mind when drafting benefits policies. In certain cases, an employer may be permitted to adopt a prima facie discriminatory standard, provided that the standard is a bona fide occupational requirement. Employers are also expected to accommodate employees up to the point of undue hardship, a standard which varies across the provinces.

5.8.1 Immigration Laws Relating to Employment

[526] According to Subsection 30(1) of the Immigration and Refugee Protection Act, S.C. 2001, c. 27 (IRPA), a foreign national may not work (or study) in Canada unless authorized to do so under the IRPA. Indeed, it is an offence under A124(1)(c) for anyone to employ a foreign national in a capacity in which the foreign national is not authorized under the IRPA to be employed. A 'foreign national' is defined under A2(1) as a person who is not a Canadian citizen or a permanent resident, and includes a stateless person.

[527] The Immigration and Refugee Protection Regulations, SOR/2002-227 (IRPR), implemented pursuant to the IRPA, defines 'work' under section 2 as an activity for which wages are paid or commission is earned, or that is in direct competition with the activities of Canadian citizens or permanent residents in the Canadian labour market. Almost all employment-related activity would be considered 'work' within the meaning of the IRPR, and foreign nationals would therefore require some form of authorization in order to engage in such activity.

5.8.2 Work Authorization Generally

[528] There are many forms of work authorization recognized under Canadian immigration law, and not all forms require a full work permit. By way of example, a foreign national may be authorized to work in Canada without a work permit in the following circumstances: (1) as a business visitor, (2) as an international student working off campus, (3) as an international student transitioning to a work permit, (4) as a provider of emergency services, and (5) as an executive, manager, or highly-skilled worker for a short duration.

[529] Nevertheless, when a foreign national intends to provide a service for the benefit of a person or entity based in Canada, a work permit is normally required. With few exceptions, this is the case regardless of the source of remuneration or duration of stay in Canada.

[530] A work permit may be issued under either the Temporary Foreign Worker Program or the International Mobility Program. There are a number of different categories of work permits issued under these programmes.

5.8.3 Temporary Foreign Worker Program

[531] The Temporary Foreign Worker Program (TFWP) is administered by Employment and Social Development Canada (ESDC). In order to employ a foreign national under the TFWP, an employer must first obtain a positive Labour Market Impact Assessment (LMIA), previously known as the Labour Market Opinion (LMO). Following a successful application to ESDC under the TFWP, a foreign national will become eligible to seek a work permit pursuant to the positive LMIA.

[532] The LMIA is generally regarded as the most time-consuming, labour-intensive, and difficult process for seeking a work permit. This is certainly the case when considering a potential application under the TFWP's two generic categories; the High-Wage Stream and the Low-Wage Stream. The appropriate choice between these two streams depends on whether the wage offered to the foreign national falls above or below the median hourly wage determined for the destination province or territory.

[533] The High-Wage and Low-Wage LMIA Streams usually require the employer to demonstrate that it has tested the labour market (via mandatory advertising and recruitment efforts) and that despite these efforts, the employer was unable to locate a qualified Canadian citizen or permanent resident to fill the open position. Indeed, this demonstrated lack of local talent is intended to establish that the employer has no choice but to hire the desired foreign national. In other words, ESDC will only agree to issue a positive LMIA when satisfied that no qualified Canadian citizens or permanent residents have been identified.

[534] Conversely, the Global Talent Stream, a relatively new LMIA stream, does not require a test of the labour market. Briefly, this stream is intended to support either: (1) an innovative employer that requires a unique and specialized foreign national in order to scale-up and grow its operations, or (2) an employer that needs to fill an in-demand highly-skilled position which appears in a list of select, predetermined occupations.

[535] Other LMIA streams include: (1) the Academic Stream for employing certain foreign academics at degree-granting post-secondary educational institutions, (2) the Seasonal Agricultural Worker Program (intended for the employment of agricultural workers from Mexico or participating Caribbean countries), and (3) the Agricultural Stream (intended for the employment of agricultural workers from any country).

5.8.4 International Mobility Program

[536] The International Mobility Program (IMP) is regarded as far more facilitative than the TFWP, and it allows an employer to hire a foreign national under a wide variety of LMIA-exempt work permit categories. Seeking an LMIA under the TFWP is normally only considered in cases in which a suitable LMIA exemption is unavailable. The bases for LMIA-exempt work permits include (but are not limited to):

- Various international agreements under R204(a), such as the Canada-United States-Mexico Agreement (CUSMA) [which replaced the North American Free Trade Agreement (NAFTA)], the Canada-European Union Comprehensive Economic and Trade Agreement (CETA), the General Agreement on Trade in Services (GATS), and the Comprehensive and Progressive Agreement for Trans-Pacific Partnership (CPTPP).
- Various Canadian interests as defined in R205.

[537] There are more than fifty LMIA-exempt categories of work permits available under the IMP. A brief description of two commonly used LMIA exemptions will be provided here.

[538] The intracompany transferee (ICT) exemption applies to foreign nationals employed by multinational organizations, who are transferring to a related entity in Canada. The general ICT work permit categories for executives/managers (C62), specialized knowledge workers (C63), and employees starting a new branch or affiliate in Canada (C61) are all issued pursuant to the GATS. However, similar categories of LMIA-exempt work permits (with some variation) are also available under other international agreements, such as the equivalent exemptions for citizens of the United States and Mexico under the CUSMA.

[539] The CUSMA Professional (previously the NAFTA Professional) exemption is another popular category of LMIA-exempt work permit. This exemption, available only to citizens of the United States and Mexico, is intended for a foreign national seeking to engage in pre-arranged employment in Canada, and only in one of the professions identified in Appendix 2 to Annex 16-A of the CUSMA. Similar Professional categories of LMIA-exempt work permits (with some variation) are also available under several other international agreements.

5.8.5 Potential Consequences of Corporate Restructurings

[540] A corporate restructuring of any kind may have significant implications for the employment of a foreign national. This often occurs when the foreign national holds a work permit that only authorizes employment with a specified employer (known as a 'closed' work permit).

[541] On the other hand, an 'open' work permit authorizes a foreign national to work for any employer in Canada. All work permits issued under the TFWP are closed. Although most work permits issued under the IMP are also closed, there are

several LMIA exemptions that result in the issuance of an open work permit. A corporate restructuring is unlikely to have significant implications for the continued employment of a foreign national who possesses an open work permit.

[542] Following a corporate change, a primary consideration is whether the restructured (or perhaps, entirely new) entity can be deemed a 'successor-in-interest' to the original employer entity. Where a restructured or new entity assumes the role of employer, this entity must qualify as a successor-in-interest in order to continue employing the foreign national.

[543] To qualify as a successor-in-interest, the new entity must be able to demonstrate that it has substantially assumed both:

- the assets and liabilities of the original entity (e.g., cash, investments, receivables, inventory, property, human resources, etc.); and
- the interests and obligations of the original entity (e.g., accounts payable, short-term debts, advances from customers on contracts, accrued compensation, long-term lease obligations, deferred income tax liabilities, warranties, etc.).

[544] In cases where a new entity does not qualify as a successor-in-interest, a closed work permit naming the original entity will not authorize the foreign national's employment with the new entity. Instead, the foreign national will be required to obtain a new work permit in order to take up employment with the new entity. Where an appropriate category of LMIA-exempt work permit is unavailable under the IMP, the new entity may also need to go through the process of obtaining a new LMIA on the foreign national's behalf.

[545] Corporate restructurings can often interfere with the continued employment of intracompany transferees in particular. One of the primary requirements of the ICT LMIA exemptions is the existence of a qualifying relationship (i.e., parent, branch, subsidiary, or affiliate) between the Canadian employer and the foreign employer from which the foreign national was initially transferred. Should this qualifying relationship cease to exist due to restructuring, the foreign national's employment would no longer be authorized.

[546] Corporate restructurings have significant implications not only for the foreign national but for the employing entity as well. When undergoing such a restructuring, employers must re-evaluate whether the continued employment of foreign national workers will be authorized. Indeed, as discussed above, employers must be mindful that employing a foreign national who does not possess the requisite authorization will normally constitute the commission of an offence under the IRPA.

6 FUTURE DEVELOPMENTS

[547] A notable development that is beginning to impact the environment for M&A in Canada is the rapid growth of the artificial intelligence ('AI') industry. The AI industry raised more than USD84 bn in venture financings in 2021 – almost double the amount raised in 2020 – and created over USD166 bn in value through IPOs and M&A. This rate of adoption makes it essential for M&A participants to educate themselves on unique AI structuring and regulatory considerations moving forward, to ensure that transactional documents capture AI-specific nuances and protect their clients' interests.

[548] M&A participants must consider AI businesses' unique characteristics throughout the acquisition process. Early stages of the M&A process that are primarily geared toward target due diligence must be designed to accurately assess an AI company's value and risk profile.

[549] Unlike traditional software M&A, where the primary IP asset is often the software code itself, the main driver of value for an AI company is often either their 'data moat' – the company's ownership of, or exclusive right to, underlying datasets – or the proprietary model(s) developed by the company to manipulate that data. Accordingly, buyers must tailor due diligence questions and review to understand the way in which an AI company develops and utilizes its pipeline of data inputs and outputs.

[550] Buy-side due diligence on AI companies should be bolstered with enhanced consideration of IP matters. Buyers should compile a detailed list of all target IP assets, such as patents, trademarks, domain names, copyrights, service marks, and applications, as well as document non-patented proprietary information like trade secrets, processes, and programmes. Buyers should also investigate how the AI company acquires its training data, leverages relationships with third-party technology service providers, and exercises ownership rights over its product or service, and associated inputs and outputs.

[551] While understanding the AI technology stack is a critical aspect of due diligence, buyers must also contend with ongoing regulatory developments that will inevitably influence an AI company's ability to operate, which may in turn have a considerable impact on target valuation and risk profile. Copyright and data protection regulations are two areas that will likely have a major impact on the development of the AI industry.

[552] M&A participants must keep a close eye on developments in copyright because of the law's ability to influence an AI company's claim over data inputs or outputs. Depending on the terms and conditions of the source and the way the data is acquired, the target company may have limited or no rights to use, modify, share or transfer input data for the purposes of its AI business. The output of the AI system may also contain data protected by copyright or other statutory provisions, which may expose it to various liability risks under copyright law, such as claims for infringement, damages, injunctions, disclosure or destruction. These risks could affect not only the target but also the buyer, who may assume the target company's liabilities after completion of the M&A deal.

[553] Buyers must also review how the company collects, stores, processes, and protects personal data to determine whether an AI company complies with relevant privacy laws and local data protection regulations. M&A buyers should consider what systems and processes the target has in place to oversee its use of AI and the challenges posed by such technologies. Since the AI regulatory landscape is changing, it is important to examine the target company's organizational supports and systems for not only compliance but also the ability to adapt to the evolving regulatory landscape.

[554] As much as adapted due diligence is key in AI M&A transactions, so is the careful drafting of foundational transaction documents. The drafting of foundational transaction documents requires careful consideration and classification of the definitions, reps, warranties and other contractual terms governing the inputs and outputs of the AI model(s), including any fine-tuning of proprietary datasets by the third-party software companies that are often the main customers of such AI companies.

[555] Definitions must be accurate and broad enough to capture the full value of the AI target company, inclusive of all the technology assets, inputs and outputs owned by the target. Clear ownership provisions are essential given that various components of AI systems may be protected by different forms of IP. Buyers must ensure they acquire all necessary rights to use these systems in order to protect their interests in underlying assets.

[556] Representations and warranties must be tailored to address the unique risks associated with AI companies, which may not be sufficiently captured by boilerplate language in traditional transaction documents. M&A participants should pay careful attention to the risk profile of the AI company, and its capacity to produce high-risk outputs when drafting provisions designed to mitigate risk and allocate responsibility for the use of AI tools.

[557] Indemnities will also be an essential, and highly negotiable, element of AI M&A deals moving forward, as M&A participants aim to allocate liability effectively in the context of an evolving regulatory landscape. Buyers should consider drafting indemnities to protect themselves from third-party claims like IP infringement or unauthorized data use.

[558] Ultimately, AI M&A demands specialized due diligence and tailored transactional documents to appropriately capture value, mitigate unique risks, and ensure successful dealmaking. While AI has been around for a while, recent developments have increased pressure on M&A participants to be mindful not only of the law as it stands but also of ethical considerations and political discourse that can hint at where the law is going, in order to best protect in the interests of parties to an AI M&A transaction in Canada and globally.

www.ingramcontent.com/pod-product-compliance
Lightning Source LLC
Chambersburg PA
CBHW071348230926
51846CB00002B/478
* 9 7 8 9 4 0 3 5 1 2 0 9 9 *